A Pictorial History of
Leigh Harriers A.C

"This book is dedicated to those local sportsmen and women who achieved greatness at their chosen event, also to the people who through their dedication have made Leigh Harriers & Athletic Club what it is today. They include trainers, officials and supporters, and those athletes who did not quite make it to the top, but gave their all when needed."

John Taylor

The author pictured running in the World Masters 10k Road Race, Auckland, New Zealand, April 2004.

LEIGH ATHLETIC GROUND AS IT APPEARED IN 1892

Drawn by the author John Taylor in 1972.

Leigh Harriers & Athletic Club
Headquarters and Ground
CHARLES ST, LEIGH
LANCASHIRE

A Pictorial History of
Leigh Harriers A.C.
Photographs by R. Sutton

Richard Sutton pictured above on Leigh Harriers Athletic ground in 1936,
the year of his retirement from athletics,

Researched and compiled
by John Taylor

Collins & Darwell have been printing bill posters, sports programmes, results and membership cards etc. for Leigh Harriers and Athletic Club for over 100 years.

ISBN 978-0-9563251-0-5

Published by John Taylor

Author can be contacted at e-mail:- john.taylorpictorial@yahoo.co.uk

Printed by
The Amadeus Press, Cleckheaton, BD19 4TQ

CLUB BADGE

....Foreword...

Quoting from Edwin Roberts book, "50 Years of Athletics", published in 1959, the following is still relevant :-

"In trying to compile a history of athletics, it is not possible to include all who have been members of the club, and no disrespect is being shown by only including those who have figured prominently in championship events. No club could exist without the athletes who turn up year after year, knowing they will never see their names in the headlines."

(Edwin Roberts Ex-Sprinter & Harriers Secretary)

Edwin (Teddy) Roberts (1902-64) on his marks, in set position, at the Leigh track in 1930.

Leigh Athletic Club – The Beginning 1888

On the 1ˢᵗ December 1888, a goodly muster of members and representatives of the Atherton and Tyldesley cycling clubs, met with the newly formed Leigh Harriers (October last), and the Leigh cycle club, at the Railway Hotel, Twist Lane, Leigh. Leigh sporting enthusiasts met with the four clubs, with a proposition of co-operating together to combine the clubs into one body, and form a new athletic association.

Mr Albert Turner of the Atherton Cycle Club, promised the support of the cycling clubs, to all the supporters who turned up at the meeting, providing the promoters would select a field for athletic purposes in a central position between the three towns, The chair was occupied by Mr Walter Bootle, Captain of Leigh Cycle Club, a code of rules was adopted, these being similar to those of the Manchester Association. Twenty new members were enrolled during the meeting and a committee of nine members was appointed, the roll contained 71 names. Mr R.Leigh was appointed captain of the cyclist division, Messrs.W.A.Howarth and W.Bootle were appointed auditors, and after considerable discussion it was unanimously resolved that the new club would be named 'The Leigh Athletic Club'. The subscription to be fixed at 2s 6d per annum, which would entitle members to participate in the privileges of the various branches of the club.

The inaugural dinner of the athletic club was held in January 1889, at their then headquarters, the Railway Hotel on Twist Lane. The landlord, Mr Joseph Glover, who kept the inn for thirty years, provided a large spread for fifty members and friends of the club. After dinner, Mr W.A.Howarth, vice-captain, proposed the toast of Leigh Athletics Club, which was responded to by Mr W.Bootle, who informed those present of the satisfactory state of the club. He remarked that the club possessed seventy five paid up members, and that it was the club's great objective to provide a good gymnasium and track for cyclists and runners. During the evening a good selection of songs, recitations, and readings were given by the members; some very funny songs given by Sammy Buttercup of the Leigh Chronicle caused great amusement. Mr O.S.Quigley, who was captain of the club, sang Dutch songs with Tyrolean choruses which were much admired. Mr James Battersby's comic songs were also very well liked. A dozen other members gave their solo acts, the talent being first class. The party broke up shortly before eleven o'clock, and the usual votes of thanks were given by the members.

Reproduced courtesy of Wigan Heritage Service.

This Edwardian photograph shows the Railway Hotel on the corner of Findlay Street and Twist Lane, which was the headquarters of the Athletics Club in the late 1880s. The name above the door is that of Joseph Glover, who was the licensee of the hotel at that time, he died whilst landlord in 1911.

OBTAINING THE NEW GROUND

On a Monday evening, 3rd March 1890, a general meeting of the Athletics Club was held at the Lilford Hotel, where Mr James Battersby presided over a large attendance to discuss Lord Lilford's offer of a 4½ acre field at the lower end of Charles Street. The field in Leigh/Atherton, known locally as Trough-Meadow, was where the defunct Agricultural Association had held their exhibition shows for a number of years, the first one in 1882.
It was resolved that the offer be accepted and his Lordship agreed to lease the field to the club for a period of 14 years at a rent of £20 per year. He also promised to lend the club £150 free of interest towards the cost of fencing the field and making a footbridge over the Atherton brook, which would form the only entrance onto the ground.

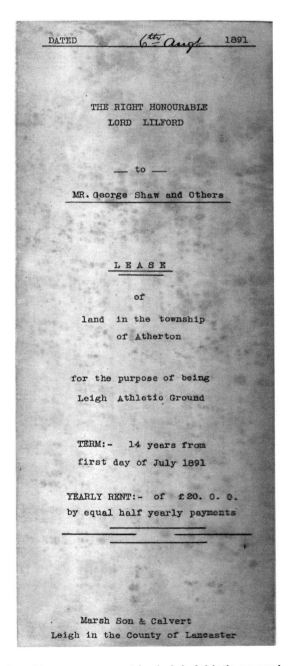

The agricultural society held their exhibition shows in the 1880s on the Old Trough Meadow field, which was to become the new athletic ground in 1891, entries for the shows were: implements, livestock, produce, poultry, pigeons, dogs, local turnouts and tenant farmers' one-day exhibits.
The agricultural society was re-constituted in 1893

Land lease agreement for Leigh Athletic ground, dated July 1891, signed 6th August 1891

Committee and Members of the Athletic Club 1888-1898

1. Dr.E.A.Doyle. | 2. Robert Horrocks. | 3. James Thorp. | 4. George Shaw.
5. James H.Stephen. | 6. Caleb Owen. | 7. William C.Jones. | 8. Rev.E.F.Crosse.
9. Thomas W.Travers. | 10. John Boydell. | 11. W.H.Pennington. | 12. John H.H.Smith.
13. Jonathan Dewhurst. | 14. Thomas Darwell. | 15. Albert H.Hayward. | 16. Thomas Lonsdale.

1. **Dr Edward Alexander Doyle** was president of the Athletic Club in 1888-94; he lived at Birch House, Bedford and had a medical practice in Leigh for 32 years from 1877-1909. He was a member of the British Medical Association and surgeon to the Lancashire and Cheshire Miners Permanent Relief Society. A Roman Catholic who took no active part in politics; he displayed a great interest in sport, and was a President of the Leigh R.F.C. and a Member of the Leigh and Lancashire County Cricket Clubs. He died in March 1910, aged 54.

2. **Robert Horrocks,** 1869 -1955, lived in Wood Street, Bedford, Leigh, and was the Athletic Club's first Secretary from 1888-1894. He himself was the five and ten mile club cycle champion, the Bedford Church gymnasium champion and captain of the swimming club in the 1890s. He had the honour of being chosen as one of the Special Guards of Honour to Queen Victoria when she opened the Manchester Ship Canal 21st May 1894, and was one of the representatives of the Battalion at her funeral in January 1901. During the Great War, Mr Horrocks served in the recruiting office on Bradshawgate, Leigh, before enlisting into the Lancashire Fusiliers as the Musketry Instructor, and attained the rank of Sergeant Major. He received a Long Service Decoration for the Volunteer Force and Territorial Army. He was succeeded as the club's Secretary by O.S.Quigley in 1895, followed by J.R. Woodward in 1896.
He died in February 1955, aged 85.

3. **James Thorp J.P.**, Vice President in 1890, lived at Stone House, Pennington, and later at Holly Bank, Orchard Lane. He was the Managing Director of his uncle's mills, J.J.Hayes's Victoria Spinning Mills. He declined to be the first Mayor of Leigh; however he was provisional Mayor in the Charter of Incorporation in 1899, and was a J.P. for Lancashire. He accepted the Presidency of the Leigh Lifeboat Society in 1896, he died Feb 1914, aged 73.

4. **George Shaw**, Vice President in 1890; later became President in 1909. He resided at Pennington Hall, and was owner of the brewery in Guest Street, Leigh. He became the second Mayor of Leigh in 1900. A member of the Marquis of Lorne Lodge in 1888 and Worshipful Master in 1901. He died June 1918, aged 58

5. **James Henry Stephen**, Vice President 1890-91; a mining engineer and land surveyor, born in Bradshawgate, Leigh in 1858. He was one of the founders of Leigh Literary Society in 1878 and became President in 1898-99. He played a big part in the development of his native town, and amongst other projects assisted in the laying out of the Leigh and Atherton joint sewerage boards works, the building of the Astley sanatorium, the Technical School and Public Library and Leigh Savings Bank. He was agent for several large estates, and it was his fondness for the Lake District which led him to christen streets in Leigh with such names as Coniston Street, Ulleswater Street, Langdale Street etc. He was a member of the Marquis of Lorne Lodge from 1887 until his death in June 1931, aged 73.

6. **Caleb Owen**, of Clough House, Leigh, was one of the Vice Presidents of the club in 1890. He represented St Thomas's Ward Urban Council in 1898-99, and after the Incorporation of the Leigh Borough, from 1899 till 1904. He was J.P. for the Borough, appointed at the creation of the Leigh Borough Bench, and was a member of the Marquis of Lorne Lodge in 1890. He died in July 1941, aged 80.

7. **William Charles Jones**, Vice President 1890-91. He was a candidate in the Borough by- elections in 1892. Mr Jones was a generous man; he built the Butts Church Schools at a cost of over £3,000, and was a giver to the Bedford Church Gymnasium. He died in October 1909, aged 56.

8. **The Rev. Edmund Francis Crosse, F.S.S.** Ordained Curate of Bedford in 1889. He frequently turned out for the Harriers cross-country team during the 1890's, and was Vice President of the club 1890-92. He acted as referee at the opening sports of the new ground in October 1891, and was judge for the track races up to June 1892.

9. **Thomas Wilmot Travers** J.P. Surveyor, Engineer, Valuer and Estate Agent. He was a track judge at the very first track sports at the new athletic ground in October 1891, and acted as official track judge at the club sports in June 1892 and April 1893. He was made a county magistrate in April 1911 at Leigh and was a member of the Marquis of Lorne Lodge from 1887; he became Worshipful Master in 1895. He died in November 1924, aged 62.

10. **John Boydell,** Secretary of the Athletic Club 1898-1909, was the club track cycle champion in 1890. He was Director of his father's iron foundry, Wm Boydell & Sons Ltd, and was in the Leigh Volunteers and the Territorials, holding the rank of Colour Sergeant. He died at the outbreak of war, September 1914, aged 48, leaving a widow and five children.

11. **William Henry Pennington** was at the club's first annual dinner at the Railway Hotel on Twist Lane in January 1889, and acted as track judge in June 1892. He lived at Stock Platt House on Leigh Road. He represented St Mary's Ward Urban council 1894-1899, and was Alderman 1899-1905. He became a member of the Marquis of Lorne Lodge in 1877, and was Worshipful Master in 1887. He died in June 1922, aged 77.

12. **John Henry Holmes Smith** was a member of the club from the beginning in 1888, living at 36 The Avenue, Leigh, and later at Parkfield, St Helens Rd, Pennington. He became a Councillor in 1899, and a J.P. for the Borough in 1905. He was Honorary Secretary of the Leigh Literary Society for over 40 years, Honorary Treasurer of the Leigh and District Nursing Association, a member of the Marquis of Lorne Lodge from 1907 and the Lilford Lodge from 1904. He died in June 1931, aged 72.

13. **Jonathan Dewhurst** was a member of the club and acted as track judge in June 1892, and again at the Grammar School sports September 1900. He lived in Wilkinson St. Leigh, and was manager of the Leigh Theatre Royal. He was a candidate in the Borough by-elections in 1894. He became a member of the Marquis of Lorne Lodge in 1892, and died August 1913, aged 77.

14. **Thomas Darwell** was present at the annual dinner for the Athletic Club members at the Lilford Hotel in February 1891, with J.Dewhurst and J.H.H.Smith. He was a grocer on Market Street. Leigh, a candidate in the Borough by-elections in May 1903, he became a member of the new Leigh Harriers & Athletic club in 1909, and the Marquis of Lorne Lodge in the same year. He died in June 1915, aged 55.

15. **Albert Harris Hayward,** Leigh Solicitor, was elected as a Conservative on the Leigh Town Council, representing St. Mary's Ward, when it was first incorporated in November 1899. From 1905-1920, he was secretary of Leigh Infirmary. He lived in Railway Road, Leigh, and later at Fern Bank on St Helens Road. He attended various track meetings, and acted as a track judge at the last track sports of the old club, in May 1898. He was Worshipful Master of the Marquis of Lorne Lodge in 1910, and died in December 1955, aged 86.

16. **Thomas Lonsdale** was elected as a councillor for the Leigh Borough in 1901, and as a J.P. in 1903. He acted as an official during the 1890's club sports, and at the reformation of the club sports in May and September 1909. He died in February 1939, aged 79.

Lilford Crest 1888

John, Lord Baron Lilford 5[th,] pictured above in 1914, sold the ground to the club in June 1945 for £2,500. His father Thomas Littleton Powys, Baron Lilford 4th, leased the land known as Trough Meadow to the Athletic Club in 1891 for £20 per year.

Work ahead

Tuesday evening, 3rd June 1890, the Athletic club members held a meeting at their new temporary headquarters; Mr T.Armstong & Bros., Leigh Bridge Cycle Stores.
Once the negotiations and the acquisition of the plot of land in a central position of the town had been successful the club began to invite tenders for the erection of suitable hoarding around the land, and to commence work on the footbridge over the brook, also the laying of a quarter mile circular cindered track six yards broad for foot races and cycling. It was also decided that a junior Harriers be formed, the subscription fee to be 1s. 6d. per year.

Athletics Club Dinner 3rd February 1891

The annual dinner for the members of the Leigh Athletics Club was held on a Tuesday evening, at the Lilford Hotel, Leigh, where about forty persons sat down to an excellent dinner. Mr Joseph Jackson, who was a Vice President of the club and had been licensee of the hotel since 1880, catered in his usual excellent style.
After dinner, the chair was taken by Mr W.A.Howarth who, in the course of his remarks, said that everything had been settled in regards to the new ground; the lease was being drawn up, and the work of boarding the field with an eight foot high fence of vertical railway sleepers was ready to commence. The boarding had to be completed within a month, and afterwards, a quarter mile track would be laid which was expected to compare favourably with any other track in England.

The usual loyal and patriotic toasts to the club, and to future success, were drunk with enthusiasm. During the evening Mr Jonathan Dewhurst, actor, manager and lessee of the Theatre Royal, (which became Leigh Casino nightclub, demolished in 2008) recited "The Bells", "The Woman of Mumbles Head" and "Gentle Jone" in his usual powerful and dramatic style. It was followed by a substantial amount of applause by his audience. Mr W.Reddish displayed his vocal powers to advantage in "On Board the Calabar" and "The Woman Politician". Mr O.S.Quigley favoured the company with a comic song entitled "Gone Forever", Mr J.H.H.Smith sang in characteristic style "Noah's Ark" and recited "The Soldiers' Pardon", Mr J.R.Boyd gave his well known rendering of "Father Prout", Mr J.E.Beardsworth gave an excellent concertina solo, Mr A.Sutcliffe gave a song, and Mr T.Darwell rendered the topical song "Father O'Flynn". A convivial evening was spent.

The successful businessman Mr Jonathan Dewhurst, Manager of Leigh Theatre Royal, pictured with his third wife, actress Fanny Rivers. Jonathan acted as one of the Judges at the Leigh Athletic club sports, June 1892.

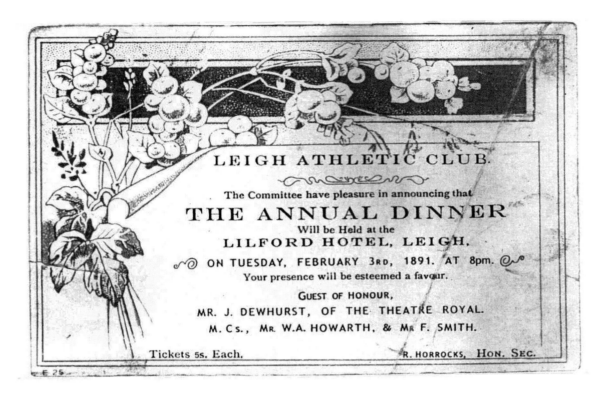

A ticket for the 1891 Athletic Club Dinner at the Lilford Hotel. The club had Mr Jonathan Dewhurst of the Theatre Royal as guest of honour. On the reverse side is the coat of arms of the hotel, and the card is made out to a Mr J.Aspinall.

Even though the number of members had risen to 100, only 40 persons actually attended the dinner. They would have been members of the committee, along with friends or partners; no doubt the only people who could afford the ticket price of 5 shillings. The majority of members would have thought the asking price too expensive, as 5 shillings would have paid a full year's subscription from November of that year.

1890-91 Members Card, which belonged to Councillor
John Henry Holmes Smith, 1858-1931.

Progression of the track

The half yearly meeting of the Athletic Club was held on a Wednesday evening, 22nd July 1891, at their new fixed headquarters, the Lilford Hotel, Bradshawgate, Leigh.

Mr J.Dumbill presided over a large attendance. Mr R.Horrocks, the Secretary, presented his report which showed that the club was in a highly flourishing condition; there was a considerable increase in the number of members, 150 at that time. It was also mentioned that the field was in a very forward state, and that it was expected to be ready by the end of September. Mr C.Rowland was appointed captain of the cycling section in place of Mr R.Leigh who had resigned, and Mr S.Wigham was appointed vice-captain. That concluded the business.

In August 1891, now that the lease had been signed, Mr R.Horrocks the secretary of the club, called a special general meeting of the members. He was anxious to get a large number of the members together, there was really no business to transact, but Mr Horrocks reminded the members that they had been very lax in their efforts to lay the running track. It was to be hoped that steps would be taken to get the track in good order for the opening of the new ground and sports, which it was proposed be held in October.

Two of the earliest known professional sprinters to run and compete on the new ground.

Sprint Champion James Green, 1869-1947   **William J. Hughlock, 1869-1940**

James Green, pictured with his trainer, was one of the first sprinters to race on the Leigh Athletics track in the 1891-92 season. James (nicknamed "Grady") was born in 1869 in Westhoughton, and lived at 4 Barn Hill until he married Edith Beetle in 1898. He raced on various grounds around the Leigh and Wigan areas during the 1890s. In December 1894 James, standing at 5ft 2½ins, raced T.Green of Warrington, at the West End Ground, Wigan. Grady had to run 115yds and T.Green 111yds. Grady won the challenge easily, and won the £100 stake money in front of 1,600 spectators.

William James Hughlock was born and died in Chorley, Lancashire. He was father-in-law to Herbert Tomblin, who was a sprinter for the Leigh Harriers Club before 1915. William is pictured above with one of his sprint trophies which he won during the 1880s. He raced on grounds from Blackburn, Wigan to Leigh, but raced and trained mostly on the Dole Lane Football Field, now known as Coronation Recreation Ground, Chorley.

Opening of the new ground, 24th October 1891

The track was 415yds round, and 6yds in width, it was excellent for either cyclist or harrier, the bends were well banked up for cyclists. The sports were to commence at 2.15pm, but at this time there was only a meagre attendance of the general public, who seemed to take very little interest in such sports, especially now that the football season had commenced. However, as time wore on, the spectators began to increase, and when the start was made about 3pm, around 500 people had assembled.
The first item on the programme was the 10-mile cycle championship, but it was decided to only race 5 miles because of the very soft ground. There were 14 entries: J.Brimelow was the winner, followed by C.Rowland and Jas Boydell.
The second event was the 100yds flat race, there were 15 entries: the winner was Mr J.Leonard. The third event, the steeplechase, provided plenty of amusement, as several of the competitors were unable to clear the steeplechase barrier and the water jump. The winner was W.M.Johnson, followed by O.S.Quigley in 2nd; Johnson was awarded a solid gold medal and Quigley silver with a gold centre. The other events were the 2-mile cycle handicap and the 5-mile Harriers Championship.
Vice President, Mr Wm.Arthur Howarth, Auctioneer & Valuer of Cook Street, Leigh, acted as official starter. All awards and prizes were presented to the winners at a dinner dance, held that evening at the Lilford Hotel, Bradshawgate, Leigh.

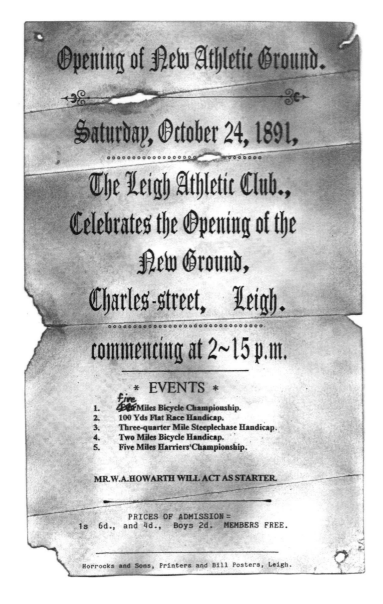

Original poster from 1891

It was decided at the General Meeting in November 1891 to raise the yearly members' fee from 2/6 to 5/-. It was also decided to have a bowling green in the centre of the field 65yds square.

Joseph Brisco, Leigh sprint-runner and professional Harrier was the eldest of eight children born to John and Esther Brisco at Wigton, Cumberland, in October 1863. His family moved to Liverpool after he was born, then to Leigh in the early 1870s, settling down at 18 Back Salford. His first race as a young man in June 1883, was at the Westhoughton Sports where he ran 2nd in a 220yds sprint. In his second race at Newchurch he ran 440yds, and came 3rd. Improving with every run, his third race was a 120yds sprint at the Tim Galvin's (ex-Leigh Rugby League Player) sports at Bucks Farm, Pennington, he easily beat the Leigh Rugby Footballers: Robin Belshaw and Sam Pendlebury.

Joe entered the ranks of professionals in 1885, at the Star Inn Grounds, St Helens, with a 300yds race, beating W. Partington of Ashton-in-Makerfield. One of his best triumphs was on the cinder track at the old Manchester racecourse, when he won the first prize in a 120yds handicap from scratch, for which there were 92 competitors. He was only beaten in three matches out of forty six races during his athletics career. He was employed as a fitter in 1880 at the Albion Iron Works, Leigh, and married Alice Southern in 1886, at Christchurch, Pennington.

At the age of 26 he was at his peak fitness, weighing 10st 4lbs and standing 5ft 6½ins tall, over a 5-year period, he won over £200 in prize money.

On various occasions in the 1880s, he was figured as a rugby player for Leigh at three quarter back position, and in 1888 he became a member of the Leigh Athletic Club, the same year that the new athletic track was under consideration. Joe became a professional starter and trainer with the club in 1893, and in April of that year he was the official starter at the club sports.

Joseph Brisco held the job of trainer to Leigh Ruby Club from August 1909, and with the Lancashire R.L. team during the 1920s. The picture above shows Joe with the Leigh players in his retirement year with the club, August 1928:
J.Houghton, T.Hurtley, J.Leyland, B.Myers, A.Worrall, J.Winstanley and A.Blackburn. Paddy Duffy succeeded him as trainer.

Joe had nine children, three of whom ran as youngsters for Leigh Harriers before the First World War. The eldest of the three, Joseph Jnr, enlisted in 1914, and was awarded the Military Medal for carrying eleven men to safety from the battlefield whilst fighting on the Western front in 1917. Whilst in Cairo Joseph played at half-back, in a rugby match for the 14th against the 13th platoon in April 1915; he kicked a goal helping his side win 8 points to 6. During his four year service, he was wounded on four occasions whilst acting as Company runner for the 5th and 11th Manchester regiments in Egypt, Turkey and then in France, he spent time recovering from his injuries at the Rochdale military hospital.

He was unable to run after the war because of his injuries. His younger brother Fred was only 21 when he was killed on the first day at the battle of the Somme, 1st July 1916, four weeks after leaving for France. When the war ended, Joseph Jnr was re-employed at the Bedford Colliery until 1922; he was then appointed as a groundsman for Leigh Rugby Football Club at the Mather Lane ground. In December 1935 whist preparing the field for the weekend match against St. Helens Recs Team, he caught a chill, and Saturday evening after the match he was taken to Leigh Infirmary with a high temperature. Pneumonia developed, his condition gradually deteriorated, and he died on Monday 9th December 1935, aged 45, he was a widower, and left two children.

In 1929, Joe retired after 50 years service as a fitter with the Leigh Albion Iron Foundry, and in June of that year he became Landlord of the Bradshawgate Inn, situated on the corner of Charles Street, (see picture). Joe gave up his licencee in his seventieth year in April 1934. In 1940, his left leg was amputated and he died shortly afterwards at his home on 27th August, aged 76. He had been a life member of the L.R.F.C. and Leigh Harriers A.C.

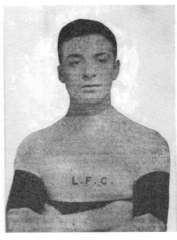  

Robin Belshaw, 1864–1927   **Joseph Brisco, 1864-1940**   **William Ewan, 1874-1928**

In April 1892, a race over 130yds on equal terms was held on the athletic ground between Robin Belshaw, ex-Leigh rugby three quarter back 1883-89, and William Ewan, Leigh three quarter back 1890-94, the stake being £10. The starter was another ex-Leigh rugby three quarter back 1884-87, and ex-sprint champion, Mr Joseph Brisco. Belshaw won by 5yds.

Joseph Bates, 1872-1924.   **George Woodward, 1863-1924**

One of the most unusual races that Joe Brisco ever started was in October 1897 on the athletic ground, between the British Ice Skating Champion, Joseph Bates of Leigh, and George Woodward, who was captain of Tyldesley Rugby Union Football Club. The event was a one-mile bicycle race both off the scratch mark for £10 aside. Bates led from the start, and won easily by 50 yards.

Joseph Bates began his skating career in 1890 and ended it in 1908. He became the British record holder and champion for the 440yds in February 1895, breaking the existing record by nearly 2 seconds in a time of 35.25sec. He married Elizabeth Whittaker in April 1898 at St Joseph's Church, Leigh. Joseph, along with his trainer R.Latham, trained on the Avenue Lake and the Plank Lane Flash in Leigh, where he broke the British record for the ½-mile straight in 1907 with a time of

1min 15.1sec. He also became the 1902 British Professional Speed Champion over a 1½-mile course. He died at his home in Warrington Road, Glazebury in July 1924, aged 52, leaving a widow and one son.

Pictured above right is veteran forward George Woodward, nicknamed "Jud Bock". He was married in Astley in 1887 to Jane Elliot. He played for Tyldesley Rugby Union Club from 1880 untill it disbanded, he then signed for the Leigh Rugby League Club in 1901. He played 19 games for Leigh, the first one against Runcorn in September 1901, and retired five months later playing as team captain for Leigh against Broughton Rangers in January 1902, after 21 long years playing both Rugby Union and League. He also played for Lancashire 1883-93, and North of England 1893-94. He became landlord of the Royal Oak, the Star Inn, and in 1901 the Jubilee Inn, which stood on the corner of Union Street and Shuttle Street, Tyldesley.

George gave up as licensee in September 1909 and emigrated to the United States, and settled in Lyle on the Columbia River, Washington Territory, where he was engaged in fruit farming and lumbering. He died suddenly on 4th May 1924 at his home in Lyle aged 61, leaving a widow and two married daughters.

LEIGH ATHLETIC CLUB.

THE FIRST

ANNUAL SPORTS

Will be held on the
CLUB'S GROUND, CHARLES STREET, LEIGH,
On SATURDAY, JUNE 11th, 1892,
Commencing at 2-30 p.m. prompt.

OVER £80 IN PRIZES.

ST. JOSEPH'S BRASS BAND will be in attendance.
ADMISSION :— 6d. & 1s. : Stand, 6d. extra.

y281

LEIGH GRAMMAR SCHOOL

THE ANNUAL ATHLETIC

SPORTS

Will be held on WEDNESDAY, JULY 4th, 1906,
on the

ATHLETIC GROUND,

CHARLES STREET. Commencing at 2 o'clock

All friends of the School are invited. It is hoped there
will be a good attendance of old boys and girls.

SELECTIONS BY THE BAND OF THE 1st V.B.M.R.

N.B.—As no Invitation Cards are being sent out this
year, friends are requested to consider this
announcement an invitation to be present.

c761

LEIGH St. JOSEPH'S CYCLING AND ATHLETIC CLUB.
(Members of the N.C.U. Under A.A.A. laws and
N.C.U. Rules.)

THE FIRST

ANNUAL ATHLETIC FESTIVAL

Will be held on the LEIGH ATHLETIC GROUND,
Charles Street, on SATURDAY, AUGUST 24th, commencing at 2-30 prompt.

PROGRAMME OF EVENTS.

1—500 Yards Scratch Cycle Race (Open)—First prize
value £7, second £2, third £1.
2—Half-mile Cycle Handicap (Open)—First prize value
£5, second £1, third 10s.
3—One Mile Cycle Handicap (Open)—First prize value
£4, second £1, third 10s.
4—100 Yards Flat Race (Open)—First prize value £5,
second £1, third 10s.
5—440 Yards Flat Race (Open)—First prize value £4,
second £1, third 10s.
6—Two Mile Cycle Handicap (Club Race)—First prize
value £2, second 15s., third 7s. 6d.

LOCAL EVENTS.

7—220 Yards Flat Race Handicap (Confined to the Leigh
Parliamentary Division)—First prize value £2 10s.,
second 15s., third 7s. 6d.
8—120 Yards Flat Handicap (Club Race)—First prize
value £2, second 15s., third 7s. 6d.
9—Football Kicking Competition (Open)—First prize
15s., second 7s. 6d.
10—Tug-of-War (Open)—First prize value £1, second
12s.
11—100 Yards Scholars' Race (for boys under 15 attending local schools)—First prize value £1, second
12s. 6d., third 7s. 6d.
Entrance Fees—No. 4, 1s. 6d.; No. 9, 6d.; No. 10,
2s. per team; Nos. 1, 2, 3, 5, 6, 7, 8, and 11, 1s.
Handicapper for Flat Events appointed by N.C.A.A.;
handicapper for cycle events, Mr. C. P. Glazebrook;
professional starter, Joe Brisco, Leigh. Full
particulars and entry forms from JOE ISHERWOOD,
hon. sec., Union Bank Chambers, or 40 Turner-street,
Leigh; also JOHN WYATT, 23 Charles Street, Leigh.
Entries close Monday, August 19th, Tuesday morning
post in time. [L163

LEIGH INFIRMARY SPORTS

FIRST AMATEUR

ATHLETIC SPORTS

On the LEIGH ATHLETIC CLUB'S GROUND
Charles Street, Leigh
Under A.A.A. Laws and N.C.U. Rules),

TO-MORROW (SATURDAY),

MAY 13th 1905 Commencing at 2-30 p.m.

BICYCLE RACES.
Event 1.—Half-mile Cycle Handicap (Open).
Event 2.—One Mile Cycle Handicap (Open).
Event 3.—One Mile Cycle Handicap (Local).

FLAT RACES.
Event 3.—100 Yards (Open).
Event 4.—220 Yards (Open).
Event 5.—880 Yards (Open).
Event 7.—100 Yards (Local).
Event 8.—100 Yards Scholars' Race (Local).
Entrance Fees:—Events Nos. 1, 2, 4, 6, and 7, 1/-;
3 and 5, 1/6 ; 8, 6d. Over 500 Entries.

PRIZES (OVER £50 IN VALUE)

Now on view at Leigh Friendly Co-operative Society's
Tailoring Shop, Central Branch.

ENTRIES CLOSE ON MONDAY, MAY 1st.

Both Cindered Tracks are in excellent condition, the
Cycle Track being well banked up.
Admission 6d. & 1s. Entrances: Charles Street
and Platt Street.
E. TRAFFORD, 4 Wilkinson-street, Leigh, and
J. A. SMITH, 43 Henrietta-street, Leigh, Joint Hon.
Secretaries. 1338

LEIGH FOOTBALL CLUB SPORTS.
(Under A.A.A. and N.C.U. Rules).

On SATURDAY, JULY 30th, 1892, the SEVENTH
ANNUAL AMATEUR

ATHLETIC FESTIVAL

WILL BE HELD ON THE
LEIGH ATHLETIC CLUB GROUND, CHARLES
STREET, commencing at 2-30 p.m.

OVER £40 IN PRIZES.

Admission, 6d. and 1s. Grand Stand, 6d. extra.
Prospectus and all information can be had from the
Secretary, JOHN QUIRK, 34, Derwent-street, Pennington, Leigh, Lanc.
REFRESHMENTS supplied on the field from 1 to 7
o'clock by Mr. Geo. Battersby, of the Railway Hotel.
a66

UNDER DISTINGUISHED PATRONAGE.

PLANK LANE CATHOLIC CYCLING AND
ATHLETIC CLUB, LEIGH.

(Members of the National Cyclists' Union and
Northern Counties Athletic Association).

Prospectus of the Second Annual

AMATEUR ATHLETIC SPORTS

(Under A.A.A. Laws and N.C.U. Rules),
to be held on the

LEIGH ATHLETIC CLUB GROUND,

Charles-street, Leigh, on
SATURDAY, the 22nd AUGUST, 1903,
commencing at 2-30 p.m.

St. Joseph's Brass Band will be in attendance.

The above advertisement for St Josephs Cycling &
Athletic club sports attracted over 400 entries in
August 1901.

Newspaper sports advertisements (1892-1906)
from the Leigh Harriers scrap books, show that the
ground was lent out to other local clubs to hold
their annual sports.

The Lilford Hotel, 125 Bradshawgate, became the headquarters of the athletic club in 1890. Mr Joseph Jackson became the manager of the hotel in 1880, and built the brewery, which was situated next to the hotel in 1895. The builder, Mr Calland performed the joinery on the brewery and Jas Battersby the plumbing, both were club members.

Many professional races took place on the athletic ground between 1891 and 1919, sometimes for considerable amounts of money.
The above picture, taken in the summer of 1910, depicts a challenge flat sprint race over 80yds for £40 between Patrick Duffy of Westleigh, on the right, and another Harrier member. Duffy won the race and the stake money by four yards.

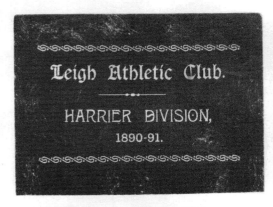

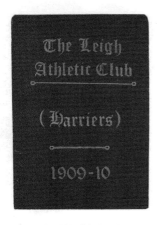

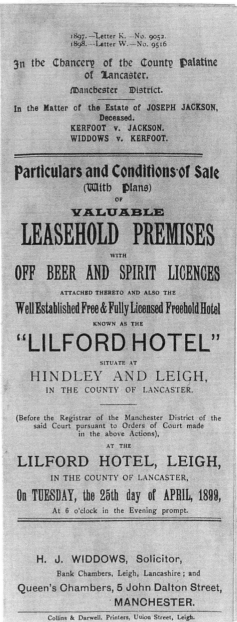

Membership cards from 1890-1930, belonging to: J.H.H.Smith, J.Dickinson, R.Sutton, and M.Thorpe, also a 1939 Northern cross country amateur athletic association members card, owned by Fred Brown. Also pictured above is the auction catalogue of the Lilford Hotel from 1896 when Joseph Jackson the licensee died at age 51. Mr W.Orrell took over the premises; he was previously of the Green Hotel at Farnworth. The athletic club had already moved two months previously to the Crown Hotel at 7 Hope Street, which was under the new management of John Leigh.

Athletic Sports on the Charles Street Ground, 22nd August 1903.

The second annual athletic sports promoted by the Plank Lane Catholic Cycling and Athletic Club, was held in beautiful weather at the athletic ground, in aid of the schools of Our Lady of the Rosary.

At 2.30pm two dense crowds gathered around the only entrance in Charles Street. The efforts of the few police and officials were ineffectual to stop the rush at the gates. The gates were broken down and hundreds of people rushed onto the ground without paying. Meanwhile a flank movement was made in the direction of Platt Street East and, whilst the attention of the police and officials were directed to stopping the rush in Charles Street, scores climbed the boards in Platt Street (now called Holden Road). It was estimated that about 6,000 spectators were present, and that out of these 1,000 gained admission without formally paying.

Throughout the various races the crowd cheered with enthusiasm. There were over 800 entries for the eleven events of running and cycling. There was a popular victory for Herbert Bennett, captain and centre three quarter and top try scorer for Leigh football club in 1903, who won the 100yds sprint handicap. Participants for the race were limited to those living within an eight mile radius of the town; Arthur Bennett his elder brother finished in third. Several spills occurred during the bicycle races, fortunately 26 members of the St John Ambulance Brigade, Leigh Division, were present. The official judge and timekeeper for the foot events was Mr J.H.Hardwick of N.C.A.A, from Salford.

Mr Joseph Brisco was the official pistol starter who lived conveniently next to the track in Sefton Street.

St Joseph's brass band played an excellent selection of music during the afternoon.

Pictured left, the official starter from Leigh, Mr Joseph Brisco.
Pictured right, Mr J.H.Hardwick, Judge and timekeeper at the sports. He was Hon. Secretary, Treasurer and founder member of Salford Harriers and a N.C.A.A. Judge and timekeeper. He was a life member of the national cross country union and became the president in 1912. Born in Mansfield in 1860 and christened John Henry, but was always known as Harry. He died in Blackpool in 1942 shortly before his 82nd birthday.

UNDER DISTINGUISHED PATRONAGE.
PLANK LANE CATHOLIC CYCLING AND ATHLETIC CLUB, LEIGH.
(Members of the National Cyclists Union and Northern Counties Athletic Association).
Prospectus of the Second Annual

AMATEUR ATHLETIC SPORTS
(Under A.A.A. Laws and N.C.U. Rules), to be held on the

LEIGH ATHLETIC CLUB GROUND,
Charles-street, Leigh, on
SATURDAY, the 22nd AUGUST, 1903,
commencing at 2-30 p.m.
St. Joseph's Brass Band will be in attendance.

Local newspaper advertisement, August,1903.

Herbert Bennett, played for Leigh Rugby from 1901 up to his retirement in 1911. He won the 100yds sprint handicap at the Leigh Sports.

Reproduced courtesy of Wigan Heritage Service

St Joseph's brass band, which musically entertained the crowds on the athletic ground during the sports, August 1903.

THE LEIGH HARRIERS & ATHLETIC CLUB FORMED 1909

The club had many members in 1909 and, at that time, was controlled by the secretary Mr John Boydell of Boydells Iron Foundry; he himself being the club's eight mile cycle champion in September 1890. He had financially supported the club and ground since May 1898, after an official ran off with a considerable amount of money from the club and left it in financial difficulty. He built the first spectator stand near to the entrance of the ground in 1898, laid new tennis courts and upgraded the bowling green on the athletic field, and paid the ground rent of 50/- a year to Lord Lilford's agent Mr J.B.Selby.

A few people who were regular competitors in those days thought there ought to be a properly organised club again, to promote sports and to have a cross county team. The first step was taken when a number of members of the athletic club, amateurs and professionals, got together and decided to promote an open sports meeting, each person guaranteed to pay his share of any loss if the sports were not a success.

Thomas Cooke was elected secretary from John Boydell, the other officials were: President Mr George Shaw, Vice Presidents: Richard Green, J.Halliwell, J.Marsh and Jim C.Seddon. Chairman John Rylance, Treasurer: William Miles Simpson. Committee: Joe Brisco, Sydney C.Bryce, W.Cox, John Joseph Davies, Albert E.Hayman, Bob Roberts, Ernest W.Walton, John Dickinson, Fred Brown and P.Ward.

The sports were held in May 1909 and were a great success. A good profit was made even after paying for a bar to be erected near the dressing rooms; the bar later became the first club house. After the sports a few members wanted to use the profits to promote further sport but, after some stormy meetings, it was decided to divide the money.

In May 1909 the headquarters of the Athletic club was the Crown Hotel on Hope Street, kept by Mr Jim C.Seddon. There was a good club room there but, after running, the athletes had to wash in a tub in the hotel's stable yard and, on one occasion, they washed in the brook after a 7-mile run. There was great enthusiasm amongst the Harriers in those days and Saturday afternoons were enjoyable; they often had hot pots provided and sing-songs after racing. In those Edwardian days other groups hired the ground from the club: The Leigh Catholic Association, Leigh Grammar School, Leigh Infirmary Sports and Leigh Rugby Football Club also promoted and held their sports there.

In July 1909, one of these sports looked like being disastrous as the ground was under two feet of water and had to be postponed for a week because the River Glaze had burst its banks flooding the Church Fields, New Platt Street and the athletic ground. A few people went around the pubs on the Friday night selling the 40 dozen pies that had been ordered for the following day.

On the 28th September 1909, the committee voted to re-name the athletic club, ' Leigh Harriers & Athletic Club'. When the Harriers had again established themselves and had money in hand, they approached Mr Boydell, and he agreed to hand over the athletic ground and contents for £50. The signatures for the club were: A.E.Hayman-Chairman, E.W.Walton-Treasurer and Thomas Cooke-Secretary. The deal was made on the 19th April 1912.`

The following year the club was told by the chairman of Lilford Weaving Company, Mr T.D.Harrison, that the ground was required for the construction of a weaving mill, and that the Harriers would have to go.

T.D.Harrison was the brother of William Harrison, Mayor of Leigh in 1908, who became Harriers president in 1912. The price was £900 and the club could not raise the money. Fortunately the site was subsequently found to be unsuitable, because quick sand was found on the site by the surveyor. The Lilford Weaving Mill was eventually built near the canal off Etherstone Street.

The club had started to build a potentially good cross country team. However, when the Great War came, everything pointed to the end for Leigh Harriers, over 40 members enlisted, including the club's Secretary Thomas Cooke. In July 1915 a few members banded together to promote professional running handicaps on the athletic ground every Friday night. All became professional by either promoting or running in the handicaps, these handicaps were a success and proved to be the salvation of the club, for it kept the members together and the club was able to pay its way.

A local newspaper advertisement May 1909, for the first open sports after the re-formation of the Athletic club, with eight events being decided and over £55 in prizes. Over 700 entries were received by the Hon. Secretary Mr Thomas Cooke, including some notable runners and cyclists from around the country.

LEIGH ATHLETIC CLUB.

SPORTS

(under A.A.A. laws and N.C.U. rules)
On the Athletic Ground, Charles Street, Leigh,
SATURDAY, MAY 15th, 1909, at 2 o'clock.
Wet or Fine.

EVENTS.	Prizes Value.	Ent. Fee
100 Yards Flat Race Handicap	£10	1/6.
220 Yards Flat Race Handicap	£8	1/6.
1 Mile Flat Race Handicap	£8	1/6.
¼ Mile Cycle Race Handicap	£9	1/6.
½ Mile Cycle Race Handicap	£9	1/6.
1 Mile Cycle Race H'cap (novice)	£4 10.	1/-

N.C.U. Definition.

| *100 Yards Scholars' Flat Race Handicap | £2 5 | -/6. |

*Open to boys attending any day school in the Leigh Parliamentary Division.

| 100 Yards Local Flat Race H'cap (8 mile radius) | £4 10. | 1/- |

Admission 6d. and 1s.; Stand extra. Tickets at reduced prices before the day of the Sports. Entry forms and all particulars from the Sports Hon. Sec.. Thos. Cooke, 29 Leigh-road, Leigh.

Newspaper caricatures of the people who took part in the May 1909 Harriers sports.

The official starter was Wm.H.'Sonny' Morton who had joined Salford Harriers from Birchfield Harriers in 1889. In 1890 he was the Northern senior cross country champion and the 20-mile world record holder in 1hr 52min 51sec, and winner of the A.A.A. 4-mile and 10-mile in 1891.

The first sports of the newly formed club had an excellent turn out some 3,000 spectators in fine but cold afternoon weather. The youngest competitor was Stanley Brisco, aged 5 years who was entered in the 100yds schoolboys' race, he was the youngest son of Joseph Brisco the well known Leigh runner. In the cycle handicap races, the young junior J.H.Wilson of Bury, competing against the senior men, had a spot of bad luck by having a spill in the 1-mile novice final and just missed out on the medals in the half mile final, but collected a silver in the quarter mile final, missing the gold by a wheel length.
There were 95 entrants in the local 100yds heats; the participants were restricted to individuals who lived within a radius of eight miles of Leigh Parish Church, the winner in the final was A.King of the Bolton Club, beating the two local club favourites F.Rothwell and J.Whittle. In the 1-mile flat race handicap open, Thomas Cooke Hon Secretary, had received 122 entries, and had them all spread out down the back straight at the start of the race, the runner who shone the most brightly was Chris Vose of Warrington A.C. passing a competitor every 10yds and winning the race easily by 15yds from F.Tonge of Eccles and L.Drinkwater of St.Helens Recs.
Mr H.N.Ellis of the N.C.A.A. was the official time keeper and judge, and licensed starter was W.H.Morton who got all the races off to a good start, and on schedule.
Edward Owen of Broughton Harriers, pictured right, winner of the 2-mile scratch inter-team invitation. Salford Harriers won the team event with 2nd, 3rd and 4th placings. Eddie (1886-1949) represented Britain at the 1908 and 1912 Olympics, setting British records at 1000m, ¾-mile, and 3,000m between 1910 and 1914.

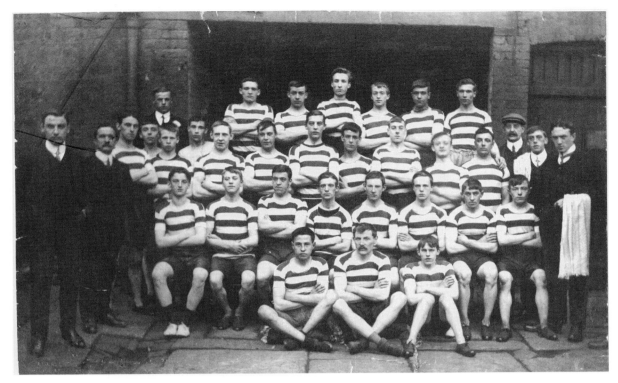

The Harriers team sitting for the camera in the stable yard of the Crown Hotel on Hope Street, Leigh, September 1909.
A couple of prominent people in the photo are:
Thomas Cooke Hon Secretary far left, next to him stands Jack Aspinall who started as a harrier in the 1880s.

Back Row: A.E.Hayman, J.Rigby, E.Silbey, S.Green, B.Holbrook, J.Sharpe, J.Talbot.
Third Row: T.Cooke. J.Aspinall, J.Corrin, J.Dickinson, H.Hindley, C.C.Abbott, F.Hodson,
                             P.Heaton, S.C.Bryce, H.Fairhurst, F.Brown, W.Ratcliffe, F.Clifton, J.Rylance
                             F.Sankey, J.J.Davies (Trainer).
Second Row: F.Calland, W.Hindley, E.Smith, W.Gaskell, F.Battersby, A.Parr, F.Rothwell, H.Unsworth.
Front Row: W.Isherwood, W.M.Simpson, J.Brisco Jnr.

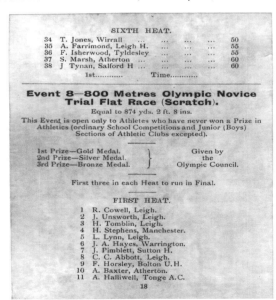

A page from a Harrier's sports programme dated 30th August 1913.

Herbert Tomblin, 1894-1949, pictured standing to the right of his trainer, was a sprinter with the Harriers Club from 1910-1914.
Even though he was basically a sprinter, he attempted to win an 800m race in August 1913 for novices, along with his club sprint
buddy Charles Clement Abbott, who later became the well-known herbalist in the area.
Herbert enlisted into the Royal Field Artillery at Leigh in March 1915, Driver L/3236. He served in the 149th Brigade D.Battalion
and fought in the Battles of Moreuil in March and April 1918, he was awarded the Croix de Guerre with Silver Star. After the war
he worked as motor mechanic engineer for Lancashire United Transport at Atherton up to his death in 1949, aged 55.

Winner of the first Harriers 1-mile open flat handicap.

Christopher Vose (1887-1970) Warrington A.C.
won the first ever 1-mile race on the Leigh track in May 1909.

He was a member of the International winning cross-country
team on five occasions for England:

1911	6th	Newport
1912	11th	Edinburgh
1913	6th	Paris
1920	2nd	Belfast
1921	4th	Newport

In the 1913 National at Wolverhampton he ran 2nd and 3rd 3 times:
1911 Taplow Court, 1920 Windsor Great Park,
and 1921 Doncaster.

He competed at the 1920 Olympic Games as a member of the
cross-country team at Antwerp, he was the 4th British runner home
in 19th position, so was not a scoring member of the British team,
who took the silver medals behind Finland.

Northern Cross Country placings

1st	1911	Haydock Park Race Course	Lancs
2nd	1913	Stockton Racecourse	Yorks
1st	1920	The Flying Grounds	Doncaster, Yorks
2nd	1921	Haydock Park Race Course	Lancs
2nd	1922	Stockton Racecourse	Yorks

and in the winning team for Warrington in 1913 ,1920, 1922.

West Lancashire Cross Country placings

1st	1913 at Lancaster
1st	1920-22 Haydock and Warrington

and in the winning team in 1913-14, 1920-23

Pictured above: As a junior, Harold Brisco was always
part of the club's cross country team up to the outbreak of the
1914-18 war. After the war he became the Harriers 100 & 220yds
sprint champion. He retired at the height of his athletic career
in the 1920s, having competed in races since he was 5 years old.

Pictured right: William Heaton, pictured at Higher Ince training
ground with one of his trainers in 1910. William was born in Wigan,
Lancs, in 1883. He ran in professional races during the late 1900s,
winning many races around the local area, with the winning stakes
ranging from £5-£50. On occasions he was entered into the Powder Hall
sprints in Edinburgh, and at one time was trained by Burgy Ben a
local trainer who was a well known wrestling champion in his younger days.

The Leigh Harriers Team 1909-10 Season
This official photograph was taken at the Church Street Gardens, now the war memorial.

1 A.Parr	12 W.Ratcliffe	23 Joseph Brisco, Jnr	34 Harold Hindley
2 F.Hodson	13 John Corrin	24 E.Silbey	35 Harry Hayman
3 F.Sankey	14 Fred Brown	25 J.Talbot	36 George Hurst
4 William Miles Simpson	15 F.Battersby	26 F.Calland	37 Jack Aspinall
5 H.Ashurst	16 W.Isherwood	27 Ben Holbrook	38 John Rylance
6 Sydney Collier Bryce	17 P.Heaton	28 J.Darbyshire	39 Albert Edward Hayman
7 F.Clifton	18 J.E.Jeffries	29 Jack Henry Sharp	40 Thomas Cooke
8 H.Unsworth	19 John Dickinson	30 H.Fairhurst	41 James Croft Seddon
9 Thomas Hurst	20 James Aspinall	31 J.Stowell	42 John Hodgson, Jnr
10 Joseph Rigby	21 W.Gaskell	32 Alf Knowles	43 Ernest William Walton
11 E.Dickinson	22 Ernest Smith	33 William Hindley	44 John Joseph Davies

Leigh Harriers track athletes group taken in 1914, at Van Asti Studio, Leigh. Only 3 names are known: standing centre is Ben Holbrook, sitting left is Charles Clement Abbott and sitting on the far right is Fred Ellison.

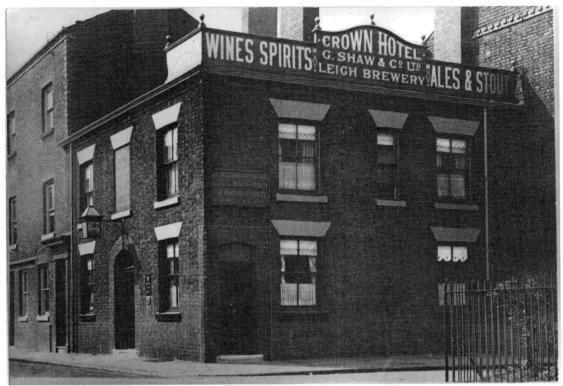

The Crown Hotel on the corner of Bond and Hope Street, Leigh.

John Leigh followed William Prescott in 1896 as the licensee of the Crown Hotel. He offered the Harriers its use as their headquarters, as did subsequent landlords of the hotel: Alfred Grundy 1907-09, James Croft Seddon 1909-13, John Leigh again for twelve months followed by Harry Brown during the war years. The Harriers continued to use the hotel as their headquarters until 1919, when they built their own club house and headquarters on the Charles Street athletic ground.

New Platt Street, which was re-named Holden Road in 1923, seen here flooded, along with the Athletic Ground on the right of the picture, July 1909. It is believed that the person rowing is Mr William Boydell, taking the driest route with a friend. Mr Boydell (1886-1976) was a club committee member from the 1920s up to 1960s, as his father had been in 1888.

Leigh Harriers hold their first major cross country championship.

The first East Lancashire & Manchester district cross country championship for junior and senior men was held at Leigh 28th Jan 1911. A thirty yard stretch of hoarding was taken down along the north side of the ground to admit the runners onto the cross country course. The teams started from their allotted pens on the athletic field, the route was well mapped out and flagged by Thomas Cooke and the enthusiastic members of the Leigh Club. A special thank you was made to Major John Baseley Selby, Mr Arthur Marsh of Old Hall Farm, and the Rev Canon Irton Smith, by whose permissions the surrounding countryside could be used for the championships.

The highest entries received were in the junior event, with over 260 athletes taking part. Walter Scott of Broughton H.A.C. won the senior race by nearly 1½ min; he represented his country in the 10k at the 1912 Stockholm Olympics, and was the A.A.A. 10-mile champion in 1911 and 1912.

Four years after the above cross country championships, nearly 400 athletes enlisted into the forces to fight in the First World War, all from the affiliated East Lancashire cross country union, 54 from the Leigh Harriers Club.

W. Scott- East Lancs Senior Champion.

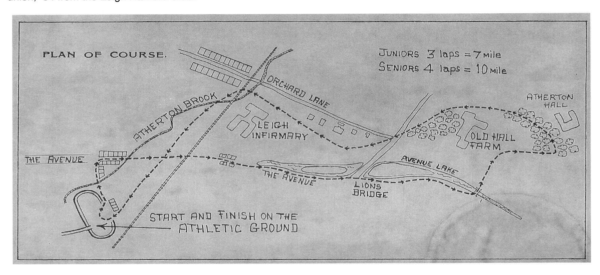

Plan of the cross country course for he East Lancashire Championship at Leigh 28th January 1911.

Mr Thomas Cooke, Hon. Sec. Leigh Harriers A.C.

Mr Arthur Marsh of Old Hall Farm

Mr Major J.B.Selby, of Atherton Hall, Land Agent to Lord Lilford.

Rev.Canon Irton Smith St Marys Parish Church, Leigh.

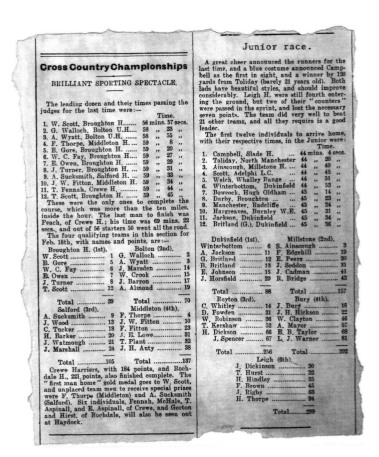

Cross Country Championships

BRILLIANT SPORTING SPECTACLE.

The leading dozen and their times passing the judges for the last time were:—

	Time.
1. W. Scott, Broughton H.	56 mins. 57 secs.
2. G. Walloch, Bolton U.H.	58 ,, 23 ,,
3. A. Wyatt, Bolton U.H.	58 ,, 55 ,,
4. F. Thorpe, Middleton H.	59 ,, 8 ,,
5. E. Gore, Broughton H.	59 ,, 20 ,,
6. W. C. Fay, Broughton H.	59 ,, 27 ,,
7. E. Owen, Broughton H.	59 ,, 29 ,,
8. J. Turner, Broughton H.	59 ,, 31 ,,
9. A. Sucksmith, Salford H.	59 ,, 33 ,,
10. J. W. Fitton, Middleton H.	59 ,, 34 ,,
11. T. Fennah, Crewe H.	59 ,, 44 ,,
12. T. Scott, Broughton H.	59 ,, 45 ,,

These were the only ones to complete the course, which was more than the ten miles, inside the hour. The last man to finish was Peach, of Crewe H.; his time was 69 mins. 22 secs., and out of 56 starters 50 went all the road.

The four qualifying teams in this section for Feb. 18th, with names and points, are:—

Broughton H. (1st).		Bolton (2nd).	
W. Scott	1	G. Walloch	2
E. Gore	5	A. Wyatt	3
W. C. Fay	6	J. Marsden	14
E. Owen	7	W. Crook	15
J. Turner	8	J. Barron	17
T. Scott	12	A. Almond	19
Total	39	Total	70

Salford (3rd).		Middleton (4th).	
A. Sucksmith	9	F. Thorpe	4
J. Wood	13	J. W. Fitton	10
C. Tucker	18	F. Fitton	23
H. Barker	20	J. E. Lowe.	31
J. Watmough	21	T. Plant	32
J. Marshall	24	J. H. Auty	38
Total	105	Total	137

Crewe Harriers, with 184 points, and Rochdale H., 221 points, also finished complete. The "first man home" gold medal goes to W. Scott, and unplaced team men to receive special prizes were F. Thorpe (Middleton) and A. Sucksmith (Salford). Six individuals, Fennah, McHale, T. Aspinall, and E. Aspinall, of Crewe, and Gorton and Hirst, of Rochdale, will also be seen out at Haydock.

Junior race.

A great cheer announced the runners for the last time, and a blue costume announced Campbell as the first in sight, and a winner by 120 yards from Toliday (barely 21 years old). Both lads have beautiful styles, and should improve considerably. Leigh H. were still fourth entering the ground, but two of their "counters" were passed in the sprint, and lost the necessary seven points. The team did very well to beat 21 other teams, and all they require is a good leader.

The first twelve individuals to arrive home, with their respective times, in the Junior were:—

	Time.
1. Campbell, Slade H.	44 mins. 4 secs.
2. Toliday, North Manchester	44 ,, 20 ,,
3. Ainscough, Millstone H.	44 ,, 40 ,,
4. Scott, Adelphi L.C.	44 ,, 45 ,,
5. Welch, Whalley Range	44 ,, 51 ,,
6. Winterbottom, Dukinfield	44 ,, 53 ,,
7. Bowcock, Hugh Oldham	45 ,, 14 ,,
8. Darby, Broughton	45 ,, 23 ,,
9. Manchester, Radcliffe	45 ,, 24 ,,
10. Hargreaves, Burnley W.E.	45 ,, 31 ,,
11. Jackson, Dukinfield	45 ,, 34 ,,
12. Britland (G.), Dukinfield	45 ,, 36 ,,

Dukinfield (1st).		Millstone (2nd).	
Winterbottom	6	S. Ainscough	3
A. Jackson	11	F. Edgehill	19
G. Britland	12	E. Pears	20
R. Britland	13	J. Seddon	31
E. Johnson	15	J. Cadman	41
J. Horsfield	29	R. Bridge	43
Total	86	Total	157

Royton (3rd).		Bury (4th).	
C. Whitley	14	J. Bury	18
D. Fowden	21	J. H. Hickson	22
W. Robinson	36	W. Clayton	46
T. Kershaw	52	A. Mayor	57
H. Dickson	66	E. B. Taylor	68
J. Spencer	67	L. J. Warner	81
Total	256	Total	292

Leigh (6th).	
J. Dickinson	30
T. Hurst	32
R. Hindley	35
F. Brown	45
J. Rigby	63
H. Thorpe	94
Total	299

Newspaper results from the East Lancashire cross country championships at Leigh 1911.
George Curtis Locke Wallach of the Bolton Club, who ran second in the senior event, ran at the 1912 Olympics in the 10K & cross country events. (B.1883 D.1980)

This photo was taken from the athletic ground gate on Holden Road, March 1930, looking across the field, which is now Charles Street, towards the Avenue, when it was still possible to start a cross country race without coming into contact with any streets.

Joseph Brisco with the Leigh R.L.team before their match against Australia, 15th Nov 1911.

In 1909, after serving for nearly twenty years as the Harriers coach, Joseph followed Jonathan Hodgson as the Leigh Rugby Team's trainer. Joseph is seen above with the Leigh team before their match against Australia, Leigh lost the match 12 points to 13 on the Mather Lane Ground, in front of 6,500 spectators. The Mayor of Leigh, Councillor Holden kicked off the match for Leigh. The Leigh Rugby League club received £271 in gate money.
Left to right back row: J.Brisco, A.Eckersley, R.Barton, J.Cartwright, H.Woods, J.Lowe, R.Gallop, Wm.Cleworth, Geo.E.Sinclair (Treasurer).
Middle row: B.Neville, M.Bolewski, T.Johnson, R.Atkinson, T.McGeiver.
Front row: A.Lee, S.Johnson, W.H.Ganley.

Thomas Hurst was born in Atherton on 12th April 1884, to George and Mary Anne Hurst. Tom ran his first race at the Leigh Harriers sports in June 1894, as a 10 year old, finishing second in the under 13's 100yds race. In 1910 Tommy won the Harrier's first 7-mile track championship and won again in 1911 and 1912. In 1913 he was the Harrier's team captain and won a bronze team medal in the East Lancs cross country championships. He retired from athletics when the war broke out in 1914 and reckoned that he had won more than £300 in prizes during his sporting career.
For forty years he worked on local colliery railways as an engine driver. He married Jessie Elizabeth Jones at Howe Bridge in October 1909. In their late 50s they opened a fish and chip shop at the bottom of Lovers Lane, Atherton and later moved to another on Chapel Street, Leigh. Thomas died a widower in July 1971, aged 87, leaving one daughter and grandchildren.

Bronze Medal Winning Cross Country Team February 1913

Left to right
Back row: Joseph Rigby (47th), Harold Hindley (107th), Fred Brown (32nd) Alf Knowles (DNF), Thomas Monks (91st), Walter Elmer (48th).
Front row: Johnny Simm (34th), Matt Thorpe (DNF), Tommy Hurst (17th), John Dickinson (13th), S.Ingram (50th) not in picture.
Rigby, Knowles and Elmer were all killed in the 1914-18 war.

The team posed for the above photograph behind Leigh Town Hall with the famous ceremonial rug in view, which many award winning local groups had their picture taken on. The team finished third in the 7-mile East Lancashire junior cross country championships at the Manchester race course on Sat, 8th February, 1913 The team reached the height of their ambition by winning a splendid set of medals against 36 teams, the improvement and determination of the lads that particular year was remarkable, because the previous year's efforts had only brought them to 14th place against 31 teams. The first man home was John Dickinson in 13th position, other placings were: 17th, 32nd, 34th, 47th, and 48th. It was a great misfortune that Arthur Farrimond was absent because the Leigh team was only 42 points behind the second club, and Farrimond meant this difference. The reason being that his previous membership had lapsed and therefore he did not qualify for the period of the championships.

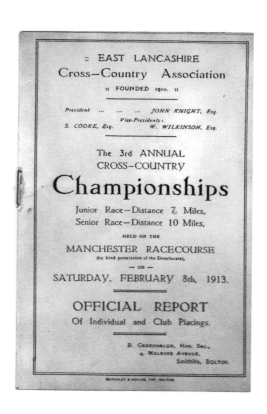

:: EAST LANCASHIRE
Cross—Country Association
:: FOUNDED 1910. ::

President ... ... JOHN KNIGHT, Esq.
Vice-Presidents:
S. COOKE, Esq. W. WILKINSON, Esq.

The 3rd ANNUAL
CROSS—COUNTRY
Championships

Junior Race—Distance 7 Miles,
Senior Race—Distance 10 Miles,

HELD ON THE

MANCHESTER RACECOURSE
(by kind permission of the Directorate),
— ON —
SATURDAY, FEBRUARY 8th, 1913.

OFFICIAL REPORT
Of Individual and Club Placings.

B. GREENHALGH, Hon. Sec.,
4, MELROSE AVENUE,
Smithills, BOLTON.

Leigh Harriers Cross Country team who became the East Lancashire Junior Champions on 13th February 1914.

Back row: J.Molyneux (trainer), H.Hindley, J.Dickinson-capt (50th), A.Farrimond (3rd), S.Ingram.
Front row: W.Rawlinson (25th), M.Thorpe (43rd), E.J.Gaffey (19th), J.Simm (34th).

Arthur Farrimond, who had the best run, set off and gradually made his way through the field, eventually finishing third, and collected a well deserved bronze medal. His team mate John Dickinson, who fell at the start of the race, hurt his ankle but still managed to finish the 7-mile cross country run at Manchester Race Course, Castle Irwell.

Leigh Rugby team 1908 on the Mather Lane Rugby Ground

The Harriers 1913-14 team was coached well by Jimmy Molyneux, the ex-rugby league half back who played for Leigh, St Helens, Swinton and county teams. He became fitness coach to the Harriers athletic team in 1910 when his rugby career ended after twenty years in the game, he is pictured above with the Leigh Rugby team when they became the first England club to beat the Australians on 28th Oct 1908. Jimmy is seated on the far left of the photo next to the Leigh rugby coach Jonathan Hodgson, whose eldest son John was a sprinter with the Harriers before the First World War.

W. R. Applegarth

(POLYTECHNIC, LONDON).

England's Champion Sprinter,

NOTABLE PERFORMANCES:

100 Yards, 9 4-5 secs.

200 Yards, 19 2-5 secs. (Record.)

220 Yards, 21 3-5 secs. (Record.)

(THE RECORD BREAKER), will compete at

LEIGH HARRIERS' SPORTS

On the Athletic Ground, Leigh,

MAY 23, 1914.

Harriers Sports Advertisement 1914

The last major sports meeting before the outbreak of war, was held on 23rd May 1914.
William Reuben Applegarth (1890-1958) was invited to run in the Leigh Sports, he was undoubtedly the best ever British sprinter before the First World War. He collected a bronze at the at 200m and Gold in the 4x100m relay at the 1912 Stockholm Olympic Games. The spectators did not grumble even though the rain came down in torrents, because they were thoroughly pleased with Applegarth's grand exhibition of speed. The Polytechnic Harrier, who finished yards ahead of the Northern and Lancashire sprint champions, ran even time for the 100yds on the muddy track.
He won his 220yds, 7th heat, in a track record time of 22.4sec but did not compete in the final because he was due to run in the 100yds handicap races. Had the weather held good, there is no doubt that the attendance at the Leigh Harriers sports on the Charles St athletic ground would have created a record crowd. When William died in 1958, he was still the record holder of the A.A.A. 220yds championship at 21.2 sec, which he achieved in 1914, this stood as a world record untill 1932.

Thomas Cooke 1884-1957, was the first Hon. Secretary of the present athletic club in 1909.

Thomas was firstly a member of Broughton Harriers then Leigh Harriers, and for a few years he was a first class sprinter with the club.
John Dickinson who followed him as General Sec for the years 1922-1953, said that without Thomas Cooke he did not think there would have been a Harriers club in Leigh. In Sept 1910, aged 26, Tom married Emily Harvey at St Peters Church, Westleigh.
In 1912 he was on the Manchester & District Committee of the N.C.A.A. Tom enlisted into the army at Leigh, Nov 1914, and was promoted to Lance Corporal in Jan 1916. Five months later whilst in the trenches with the 20th Manchesters, he was injured and lost his left arm caused by an exploding shell, his comrades who were standing by him were killed. After spending time in the Stockport then Leigh Hospitals recovering, he resumed his Hon. Secretary position with the club in 1917. He kept a diary whilst in France; a copy of it is with the British Military Museum in London. In 1922 he became more involved with the Leigh Branch of the British Legion committee as Hon. War Pensions Sec. Officer; he remained in this voluntary role up to his death in 1957. His funeral service took place at Bedford Church followed by cremation at Overdale, Bolton.

ROBERTS   LEIGH

Matt Thorpe, photographed at Van Asti Studio, Leigh in 1920, he was born in October 1889, to Matthew and Bridget Thorpe. The Thorpes had three daughters and five sons while living at Baker Street, Leigh, James and John who excelled at football, William at rugby and athletics, Edward football and athletics and Matt who took to running. He joined the Leigh club in 1910 and won his first race the following year.

In 1913 he was part of the Harriers cross country team which gained third place in the East Lancashire junior championships over 7-miles at the Manchester race course. In the same race the following year he was a member of the club's junior winning team and gained his first team gold medal.

War broke out in 1914, and gradually all five brothers enlisted, James into the Queen's Regiment and John into a Land Army Regiment. William enlisted into the Royal Scots, Lothian Reg. No 29308, and was killed in France on the 4th July 1916. Edward enlisted and served with the Royal Field Artillery as a driver.

Matt enlisted with the Lincolnshire Regiment and in July 1916 he was promoted to Lance Corporal. Unfortunately he sustained a wound to his right arm in Nov 1916, and spent time recovering in the Military Hospital at Reading, he returned to France as a Corporal.

In April 1917 he was captured by the enemy and remained a prisoner until the end of the war. He had a hero's welcome on his return to Leigh at a reception held by the Mayor, Joseph Ashworth, on the Leigh Cricket Ground in May 1919, over 3,000 soldiers attended.

Matt married Mary Garfin in September 1915, they emigrated to America in Feb 1921 but returned home to Leigh after only 15 months abroad. Matt re-joined Leigh Harriers and began winning races again; he became a good obstacle runner on the track and acquired a large collection of medals and trophies throughout the 1920s and 30s. Matt was made the Harriers Cross Country Secretary in September 1964 and was still a common face with the athletes at the Leigh club during the early 1970s.

Matt and Mary had two children, a son James Matthew who was killed at the Normandy landings in July 1944, and a daughter Marjorie. They celebateted their Diamond Wedding Annivesary in 1975, Matt died in 1981 aged 91.

Two of the Thorpe brothers: Edward of the Royal Field Artillary and Matthew of the Lincolnshire Regiment, photographed at the Van Asti studio, 41 Railway Road, Leigh, 1916.
Note their second tunic button has been blacked out; this was done in mourning for their brother William's death, who died at the Battle of the Somme, July 1916.

Pictured above are two of Edward and Matt's elder brothers James and John, who also enlisted into the land forces during 1916, James into Queen's Regiment, Regt.No.68425, and John into a Land Army Regiment.
Pictured left is their brother-in-law Ralph Garfin wearing his Royal Field Artillery drivers' uniform in 1917. He regularly turned out for the Harrier's cross country team, both before and after WW1.

Certificate of recognition awarded to Driver Edward Thorpe of the Royal Field Artillery, from the people of Leigh Borough for his services rendered in the Great War 1914-18.

These certificates were presented by the Mayor, Joseph Ashworth, at a reception in April 1919 at the Leigh Town Hall, to the Leigh and Borough servicemen who fought in the Great War.

Token of sympathy in recognition of the sacrifice of Leigh Harriers' athlete, Joseph Rigby, who was killed Oct 1917, presented to his wife, Dec 1917.

The Anchor Cable A.F.C. team were the Cable Makers Association cup winners on numerous occasions during the 1920s and 30s, photographed above in front of the B.I.C.C. bowling green pavilion in the early 1930s. The trophy can be seen in the front centre of the photograph. The only names known are: far left: Matt Thorpe, J.Evans, J.Bowyer, J.McDonnell Capt, J.Ainsworth, T.Virgo and Edward Thorpe, standing on the far right is John Hodgson, all were members of Leigh Harriers.

Medals awarded to Edward Thorpe during the First World War.
Left to right: The solid silver British War Medal, the brass Victory Medal and the Bronze 1914-15 Star.

Edward Thorpe wearing his Royal Field Artillery Horse Drivers uniform, Regt. No. 4425. He and his brother Matt were good obstacle runners at the Leigh Club; they won many valuable prizes during the 1920s. Edward was also a first class football player for the Leigh B.I.C.C. team in the 1920s and 30s.

Standing on the far left is Thomas Green, who was living on Westleigh Lane in 1914. He was Treasurer of the West Leigh Rugby Football club before the war, he is pictured above with the first team in the 1913-1914 season. After the war he acted on the Harriers committee, becoming one of the trustees of the club in July 1942.
Seated on the ground of the front row far right is William Thorpe, who competed for the Harriers track team from 1911 up to 1915 when he enlisted into the Royal Scots, 13th Battalion, Lothian Regiment as Private, Regt. No.29308. He was killed in the battle of the Somme, 4th July 1916, and is buried at Vermelles British Cemetery.

Standing on the right of the picture is George William Garfin, who was the Harrier's secretary in 1922, he enlisted into the Lancashire Fusilers 9th November 1915, Regt.No.35518, and was transferred in September 1916 to the 72nd training reserve battalion, F.Company, of the 12th Cheshire Regiment, Regt.No.58479. In April 1917, whilst fighting in Salonika he was wounded, and in March 1918 he was tranfered to the Labour Corps. Regt No.489172. George was demobed in March 1919 at Heaton Park, Manchester.

On George's left is his brother-in-law Matt Thorpe, who enlisted into the Lincolnshire Regiment on 25th July 1916. They are pictured above before being mobilised to Southampton in October 1916. Seated on the front row are three of George's brothers, who all joined the land forces during the First World War. James Thomas joined the Royal Engineers in the rank of Pioneer, Regt. No. 356967, Jack joined the Royal Garrison Artillery as Gunner Sgt, Regt. No.48339, and Ralph served in Egypt with the Royal Field Artillery. Ralph was a regular member in the cross country team at the Harriers athletic club.

Officers of the Leigh Athletes Volunteer Force at their Headquarters in Brown Street, February 1915
Back row- Messrs R.Horrocks- Acting Sergeant Major, A.H.Hayward - No 1 Platoon Commander, J.H.Prescott - Acting Instructor, E.Fitzgerald - Instructor, J.Rigby -Instructor, and W.Hurdas - Instructor.
Front row- Councillor J.Gregory - No. 4 Platoon Commander, Mr T.Mather- Company Commander, Mr T.Hunter -V.D.Officer in Command, Mr J.R.Speakman - No.3 Platoon Commander, Mr J.Bowyer - No.2 Platoon Commander.

Every Tuesday in May 1915, No.1 Platoon carried out their firing practice on the Athletic Ground; range officers in charge were Mr Hayward, Mr Bowyer, Mr Speakman, and Mr T.Mather. Company training drills were on Monday and Wednesday and full parade on Saturday. In July a second shooting range was opened by the Mayor at the Mather Lane Rugby Football Ground.

William Rawlinson, born on the 23rd January 1893 in Liverpool, was one of eight children. His father was Police Sergeant Christopher Rawlinson and his mother Alice. In 1912 as a youngster he joined the Harriers team and within twelve months he became one of the better athletes at the club, running in 1913 as a junior. On 13th Feb 1914 he received a junior team gold medal in the East Lancashire cross country championships and, in the same month, he ran 21st behind his team mate Arthur Farrimond in the Northern cross country championship at Haydock racecourse.

Up to 1914 he worked for J & J Hayes at Victoria Mills then, when war broke out, he enlisted into the Manchester Regiment with his brother John. In August 1915 he had a "brush" with the Turks when the allied troops made the memorable Suvla Bay landings at Gallipoli. His parents received a letter on the 8th May 1916, from Major.& Hon. Lt.-Col. Sidney G.Goldschmidt of the 20th Man/Regt *(pictured inset above)*, saying that Corporal Rawlinson had had the good fortune to come safely through heavy fighting in Salonika and has since been promoted to Sergeant while serving in Gallipoli. While in service he won a collection of medals whilst running for his regiment. In May 1918 he was wounded by a hand grenade which accidentally exploded injuring his left arm, stomach and thigh, he was unable to continue his running because of these injuries. His brother John was also wounded in the arm from shrapnel.

After leaving the army in 1919 he entered the G.P.O. Service and served 33 years with the Leigh Post Office, retiring as postal inspector in Jan 1953. He married Annie Whalley in September 1919, they had two children Frank and Annie. The couple celebrated their Golden Wedding Anniversary in 1969. William died the following February at his home on Warrington Road, Leigh.

In later life Major.& Hon. Lt.-Col. Sidney G.Goldschmidt became a published author of books on skilled horsemanship.

John Dickinson General Secretary 1922-1953.

Mr John (Jack) Dickinson was a member of the old athletic club 1907 and was elected on the newly formed club committee in Sept 1909. He had shown promise running with the Broughton Harriers and later with the Bolton Harriers before joining the Leigh Club in 1907. In 1913 he won the Leigh Harriers 7-mile senior track championship in record time. During the 1914-18 war he and Ernest William Walton helped to promote professional sport meetings on the athletic ground which were mainly sprint handicaps for cash prizes. The club would take a small amount of stake money from these sports and plough it back into the club funds to improve the club and its facilities on the athletic ground. Mr Dickinson was joint secretary with Thomas Cooke from 1919 up to April 1922 when he became General Secretary of the club. He was acting club Hon. Secretary for over 30 years and, during that time, he worked hard with the club's committee building up the club's facilities and grounds. During that time, as is still the case today, voluntary helpers were rarely found, however there were a few people he could rely on: Fred Brown, Matt Thorpe, William Miles Simpson, Eddie J.Simms, Edwin Roberts amongst others, and together they managed to improve the facilities and eventually buy the ground outright in 1945.

John was born in 1888 and initially worked for J &J Hayes, Victoria Mills, in Leigh. At the age of eleven he earned 2/6 per week working from 6am until 12.30pm; he then went to school until 4pm.

At sixteen he left the mill to be employed in the local coal mines, firstly at the Sovereign pit of the Wigan Coal & Iron Co Ltd., then later for Bickershaw collieries where he was employed for nearly 25 years. After 43 years working in the coal industry he retired as an engine winder in October 1956.

John married Elizabeth Moffatt in November 1911 at St Paul's Church, Westleigh and they celebrated their Golden Wedding Anniversary at their Leigh home.

The couple left Leigh for Cleveleys, near Blackpool, but after 2 ½ years they found that they could not settle and returned to their native town shortly before the club celebrated its 50th anniversary in Sept 1959. John was still a common face around the club during the early 1970s. He died in May 1974.

John Dickinson Feb 1913, the year that he won a team bronze medal in the junior East Lancashire cross country championships.

Leigh Harriers Honourable General Secretary John Dickinson, at the Leigh Sports, 19th August 1933.

Leigh Harrier's Athletes in the First World War

Driver. Edward Thorpe.
Royal Field Artillery
3rd Battalion
Regt. No. 4425

Pte. Geo Wm Garfin
Lancashire Fusiliers,
Cheshire Regiment,
Labour Corps
Reg. No. 489172
(Wounded)

Pte. Harry Ormesher
Royal Army Medical Corps.
Regt. No. 42494

Cpl. Matthew Thorpe
Lincolnshire Regt.
Regt. No. 32843
(Wounded)

Pte. Wm. Thorpe
Royal Scots, Lothian Regt.
Regt. No. 29308
Killed 4th July 1916

Pte. Arthur Farrimond
Royal Scots, 12th Platoon
1/9 Dandys C. Coy
Regt. No. 2774
(Wounded)

Lce-Cpl. Tom Cooke
20th Manchesters. A. Coy
Regt. No. 17052
(Wounded)

Lce-Cpl. Alfred Knowles
Royal Fusiliers 20th Battalion
Regt. No. 7419
Killed 17th July 1916

Sgt. Ernest Greenough
1/4th Battalion. I. Coy
Kings Own Royal
Lancasters
Regt. No. 15227
(Wounded)
Military Medal

Pte. Wm. Pemberton
Royal Welsh Fusiliers
2nd Battalion.
Regt. No. 24128
Killed 24th April 1917

Pte. Jack Henry Sharp
Sherwood Foresters C. Coy
1/6th Battalion
Regt. No. 2639
Killed 27th April 1915

W.O. John Hodgson
Army Service Corps
D. Unit. No1 Coy
Regt. No. 10384
3rd West Riding Regt.
as 2nd Lieutenant.

Sgt. Wm Rawlinson
11th Manchesters
Regt. No. 13393
(Wounded)

Sgt. Bomb.
Sydney Collier Bryce
Royal Garrison Artillery
Regt. No. 48866

Signalman.
Richard Sutton
Royal Navy
Volunteer Reserves
MZ/5367

Pte. Joseph Brisco
Manchester Regiment
14th Platoon. D. Coy
1/5th and 11th Battalions
Regt. No. 200241
(Wounded)

Pte. Samuel Green
20th Manchesters 13 Corps
Cyclist Batt. A. Coy
2nd Platoon. Regt. No. 9549.
Royal Engineers

Cpl. Ernest Smith Canadian
Army Medical Corps.
(Driver)
Field Ambulance Coy.
Regt. No. 33684
Military Medal

Sgt. William Hindley
1st Battalion
Grenadier Guards
Regt. No. 21676
Military Medal

Ernest Topping
Aircraftman 2nd Class
Royal Navy Air Corps
Regt. No. 24719
Died 30th March 1919

Pte. Harold Hindley
Royal Army Medical Corps
13th Stationary Hospital
British Expedition Force.
France
Regt. No. 35827

Pte. Fred Brisco
1st Lancashire Fusiliers
Regt. No. 29387
Killed 1st July 1916

Sgt. James Buckley
22nd Manchester Pals
5th Battalion
Regt. No. 200177
(Wounded)
Awarded the D.C.M.

Guardsman
Harry Bilsbury
Grenadier Guards
2nd Battalion
Regt. No. 21539
Killed 15th Sept 1916

Pte. Joseph Rigby
Cheshire Regt.
16th Battalion
Regt. No. 292610
Killed 22nd Oct 1917

Commissioned Officer
Lieutenant
George Eyes Hayward
Manchester Regiment
1/5th Battalion
(Trench Fever)

Pte. Walter Elmer
5th Manchester Pals & 136th
Field Ambulance Royal
Army Medical Corps
Regt. No. 69518
Killed 29th Nov 1917

Driver, Herbert Tomblin
Royal Field Artillery
149th Brigade. D. Battalion
Regt. No. L3236
**Croix de Guerre with
Silver Star (Belge)**

Bomb. Ralph Garfin
Royal Field Artillery
(Driver)
Regt. No. 86456

Pte. Sydney Kay
Manchester Regt
1/5th Battalion
Regt. No. 1542
Killed 4th June 1915

Pte. Gordon Reg Goodwin
2nd East Surrey Regt
Regt. No. 8508
(Wounded)

Staff Sergeant
John Joseph Davies
Royal Army Ordinance
Corps
Regt. No. 030875

Lce-Cpl. Fred Ellison
Royal Fusiliers
11th Battalion
Regt. No. 1311
(Wounded)

Gunner, Richard Hayes
Royal Garrison Artillery
65th Siege Battalion
Regt. No. 43656
Killed 18th May 1918

Pte. William Harvey
Grenadier Guards
4th Battalion
Regt. No. 20566
Killed 12th Sept 1916

Pte. Edward J.Gaffey
3rd Manchesters
Regt. No. 37173

Other Harrier Club Members who enlisted in the Great War

J.A.Kenyon	7th Dragoon guards - wounded.		J.Gannon	21st Manchester Pals
S.H.Kenyon	7th Dragoon guards - wounded.		F.Aldred	5th Manchesters
H.Greenhalgh	Royal Army Medical Corps		J.T.Baldwin	5th Manchesters
C.Kegan	Royal Army Medical Corps		H.Hesford	5th Manchesters
H.Mcguire	Royal Engineers		F.McQuire	Army Service Corps
E.Boyes	Royal Engineers		J.Green	Bobs Own
A.Craske	Royal Engineers		V.Smith	Royal Scots
J.W.Irville	Royal Welsh Fusiliers			

Pte. Robert Topping.
Army Service Corps
Motor Transport
2nd Battalion
Regt. No. 050086

Sgt. Harry Irlam
Army Service Corps
D. Unit, 1st Battalion
Regt. No. 136865
(Wounded)

Pte. John Wm.Hooson
Field Ambulance Coy. R.A.M.C.
B.E.F. France. Regt. No. 43471
(Wounded)
Croix de Guerre (Belge)

Rules of the Leigh Athletic Club

As Revised and Adopted March 11th, 1920.

1. That the Club be called the "Leigh Athletic Club."

2. That the object of the Club be the further development of Cross Country Running and other athletic exercises.

3. That the Annual Subscription be 4/-, due March 1st. Any member being two months in arrears with his subscription shall be liable to have his name erased from the Club's list of members.

4. That the Officers of the Club consist of President, Vice-Presidents, a Committee of twelve, and Chairman, Hon. Treasurer and Hon. Secretaries, who shall be elected annually at the Annual General Meeting, and nominations for same must be sent to the Hon. Secretaries not later than seven days prior to the said meeting.

5. That candidates for membership be proposed and seconded at any Committee or General Meeting, such candidates having previously filled up the printed application form which must be accompanied by the amount of the season's subscriptions.

5a. That candidates for Committee or Officials must have twelve months' membership.

6. That a List of Members with the amount of their subscriptions shall be placed in a prominent part of the Clubroom.

7. That the Committee shall meet from time to time to transact business as required by the Secretary, and seven shall form a Quorum.

8. That the Club's Grounds shall be accessible to members at any time, except Sunday, for training purposes.

9. That any member may personally introduce a friend into the Club on week-days, but the same gentleman must not be introduced more than four times in any one year; and any member introducing a friend must sign his name and the name and address of visitor in a book provided for the purpose and kept in the Bar.

10. That any member found guilty of refractory or ungentlemanly conduct, making use of obscene language or of violating the rules or bye-laws in any manner or form, shall be dealt with as the Committee deem advisable.

11. That no rule be made, altered or rescinded, except at a General or Special General Meeting. Notice of proposed alteration must be given to the Hon. Secretary at least fourteen days before the date of such meeting.

12. A Special General Meeting may be convened upon a requisition signed by ten members specifying the business for consideration, and no other business shall be transacted at such meeting.

13. That a dispute arising at any time shall be left to the Committee to decide.

After the war in 1919, the rules of the club were revised, and have hardly changed over the last 90 years.

After the 1914-18 War

At the end of the war sport was resumed and members who had turned professional applied for reinstatement as amateurs. The only one to be refused was Mr John Dickinson, the reason given by the Athletic Association was that he had been too prominent as a professional, and so he was made an example of, thus taking the rap for all who had turned professional.

Mr Thomas Cooke, who had resumed his Hon. Secretary position in 1917, realised that better facilities were required; in 1920 he secured one of the large billet huts from the P.O.W. camp in Etherstone Street. Weeks of voluntary work by the members saw the billet erected on the athletic ground and put to use as a clubroom. In 1922 another hut from the old P.O.W camp was purchased, the total amount for the hut, transporting and erecting on site next to the existing building, was £54.16s.8½d.

On the far left (and inset) is Sgt.Harry Irlam of the A.S.Corps who won the Harriers 1,000yds race, 16th August 1919, he had been fighting in France since 1916 and had come through the war with only a minor injury. Standing next to him are two men from Atherton, Sgt.Ernest Greenough who ran second, and standing centre is S.Marsh who ran third, right of him is Cpl.Ernie Smith. The following year Marsh, Greenough, Irlam and S.Ingram (not pictured) all joined Salford Harriers. Irlam became the Northern Counties A.A. 880yds champion in 1921, at the age of 30. Ernie Smith became a Canadian Citizen.

The first sports festival promoted by the Harriers since the outbreak of war attracted over 2,000 spectators to the Charles St Athletic ground, with 3 hours of entertaining sport. The enthusiastic band of officers who had kept the club going during the long years of war worked hard to make the revival a success. There were nine events in the afternoon programme; considerable interest was taken in the attempt at the high-jump by B.Howard Baker of Liverpool, who successfully cleared a height of 6'2", to win the Northern Counties Championship.

The best event of the day was the final of the 500yds cycle handicap, which was a close tussle between W.Rowe of Wigan and F.W.Pollard of Leigh A.C. They were both given the same time of 37.4sec, and the judge's decision was in doubt of the winner. The spectators were so keenly interested in the finish of the race that in their excitement the fencing gave way, but was soon rendered safe again. Rowe was eventually awarded first place.

The 440yds obstacle handicap only served to prove what an expert in that kind of race Matt Thorpe was, he had plenty to spare both in the opening heat and in the final, and recorded a very popular victory. Tommy Hurst finished second and Eddie Thorpe was third; all were members of Leigh Harriers A.C.

There were only five competitors out of twelve entries for the 1,000yds club championship, each man ran from scratch, a surprise defeat of Greenough, who was overtaken by Irlam, the Patricroft runner, who finished in great style, breaking the club record in a time of 2min 26.2secs, he also won the event the following year.

Other events were: the 70yds scholars' handicap, won by P.Gorman of Leigh, the 100yds open handicap, won by S.Royal of Man A.C., the 220yds open handicap, won by S.Siddal of Warrington A.C., and the 1-mile flat race by T.Jones of Sefton Harriers. A.E.Hayman, the N.C.A.A. starter, got the competitors off the mark well and kept the programme up to the schedule time. The officials performed their work in a satisfactory manner; prominent amongst them was Police Supt. Yates. During the afternoon selections of music were played by the St Joseph's band.

LEIGH HARRIERS' SPORTS.
───
(Under A.A.A. Laws and N.C.U. Rules.)
TO-MORROW (SATURDAY),
ATHLETIC REVIVAL
ON THE ATHLETIC GROUND.
OVER 400 ENTRIES,
Including Many of Our Best Athletes.
HOWARD BAKER ENGLAND'S CHAMPION HIGH JUMPER. WILL ATTEMPT TO BEAT THE RECORD.
ADMISSION: 1/- & 1/6. including tax.

The first sports advertisement after the War, as it appeared in the local Journal, August 1919.

Matt and Eddie Thorpe in the Leigh Harriers hooped shirts on the right of the picture.
On either side of Matt are Ralph and George Wm.Garfin and, lying down in the front of the photograph, is James Vincent Jones. The photo was taken after they had been competing at the Leigh Harriers Sports in August 1919.

Members of the Leigh branch of the St John Ambulance Brigade, who were on hand at the Leigh Harriers sports revival, Saturday 16th August 1919.

British army officers and guards outside the sergeants' mess on the Etherstone Street. P.O.W. camp, 1918. The two thousand German P.O.W.s, many of whom had been captured during the great battle of Mons, were housed in the newly built Pennington Weaving Mill. Above is one of the two billets which were bought by the Leigh Harriers club after the war in 1920 and used on the athletic ground as a club house and athletes' changing rooms.

Leigh junior athletic amateur football team pictured on the athletic ground in 1916.
On the front row far right is young Jack Molyneux, who later became captain of the junior and senior team in 1920, when the club won the Shaw cup.

Jimmy Rowland with his trainer F.Calland, 1919.

Jimmy was born in April 1902, he joined the Leigh Harriers as a youngster and became one of the best young sprinters during and after the First World War. He ran in all the professional organised sprint races on the Leigh track and won money prizes, of amounts between £2 and £5. He also played for the Marsland Green, Astley,senior football team and, later in life, became a local bowling champion.

As a teenager during the Great War 1914-18, Jimmy helped run a bakery shop with his father on Chapel Street, Leigh.
It was his job to take care of the family firm's delivery horse, Dora, until she was commandeered by the army for service on the Western Front. He had a picture of her stitched into his best running vest, as shown in the photograph.
Jimmy married Mary Zylinda Hitchen in Sept 1922 and, from 1939 up to his death in June 1963, he ran a local confectionary shop on Chapel Street near Butts Bridge.
Jim's father, also named James, won the 100yds sack race at the Leigh R.F.C. sports June 1891. He was also one of the training partners of Joseph Bates, the British ice skating champion and local hero back in the 1890s and 1900s.

Leigh Harriers cross country team, pictured on the Charles Street ground, prior to their last cross country run of the season, April 1920.

The Leigh Harriers team gathered for the last run of the season's fixtures, 1st March 1922, pictured above against the old cotton mill wall in Charles Street, prior to the clubs consolation handicap.
Mr Tom Cooke the club Secretary dispatched the runners from the ground and they headed in the direction of the infirmary, watched by a fair number of spectators. Richard Sutton started on scratch, conceding starts up to 4½ min, the distance of the race being about five miles through town and country, Geo.Wm.Garfin was leading at the half way mark but R.Sutton took the lead towards the end of the race from the Railway Road train station, he continued to lead through the chuchyard and along Church Street back to the athletic ground and won in a good time of 33mins. C.Gregory was 2nd and James Vincent Jones 3rd.

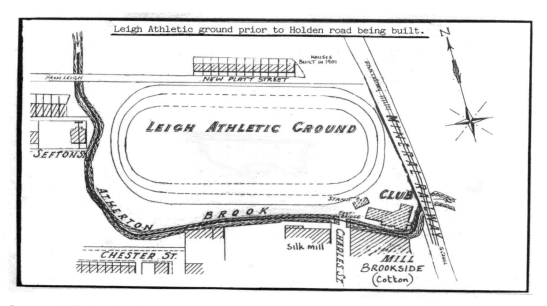

In October 1923, the Club Secretary and Treasurer attended a meeting at the Leigh Town Hall with the new roads committee. The corporation explained their wish to take a strip of land at once from the north side of the athletic ground, for the construction of a new road. A further meeting was arranged at Atherton with the Right Honourable John Baron Lilford's agent, Mr Robinson.

Mr Bamber, Leigh Town Clerk, also attended to discuss the terms to purchase the land and the possible compensation to the club. Eventually all parties were happy with the agreed terms which were, that the Corporation erected a new fence eight feet high along the whole length of the athletic ground and supply the club with ashes and lend rollers etc. for the purpose of altering and making the new portion of the track. The whole cost of the road was £53,000. It was designed to take the traffic away from Chapel Street and Bradshawgate. The name Holden Road was chosen because the Holden family had achieved two mayors in the Leigh Borough in 1911 and 1920.

Tyldesley Rugby Union Team, November 1923.

Back row: J.Lewis, R.Lewis, G.Smith, R.Carr, J.Roberts, S.R.Cheetham, J.Hunt
Second row: S.Sims, James Quinn, John Hodgson (Capt), W.E.Dowling, F.Fearnley, G.A.Wright,
Front row: H.Blood, C.Buffey.

James Quinn and John Hodgson were two of the Harriers' most prominent sprinters before the Great War of 1914-18. John Hodgson, was also a member of the Leigh Nomads A.F.C. before enlisting into the Army Service Corps as a Private in September 1914. He very rapidly received promotion to Acting Quarter Master Sergeant; this was as a result of an examination held at Aldershot in October of the same year. After approved service he was promoted to Warrant Officer in February 1915 aged 21, he was one of the youngest in H.M.Land Forces to hold this post. On the 23rd June 1915 he was posted to France with the B.E.F. and on 30th January 1918 he was commissioned to 2nd Lieutenant into the 3rd Battalion West Riding Regiment. The last time he was sent overseas was 31st July 1918 and, one week later on 7th August 1918, he joined the 13th Battalion, 178th Brigade, 59th Division of the West Riding Regiment. He was being recommended for advancement in the army when the war ended. John joined the Marquis of Lorne Lodge, Leigh in 1930, and became Worshipful Master in 1943. He died in Grange Street, Leigh in 1961 age 67. After the War, in 1920 John Hodgson and James Quinn joined the Tyldesley Rugby Union Club, pictured on the previous page; John was appointed Captain and James played at three quarter centre position.

James served his time during the war down the coal mines around the Leigh area. In 1922 he was working for Messrs. John Speakman & Sons at Woodend Pit in the Bedford area of Leigh. On the 21st January 1926 at 1.30pm a roof fall in number 3 tunnel east at the Woodend Colliery completely buried James Quinn and his mining partner James Keen. It was not until the following morning that the rescue team managed to recover their mutilated bodies. After the funeral James was buried at Leigh Cemetery, where practically all the members of the Tyldesley R.U.F. team were present, together with officials of the club. Four playing members acted as bearers, Dowling, Fearnley, Mayor, and Tickle; the wreath from the rugby members was in the team colours of blue/ white. Seventeen members of the Harriers Committee were also in attendance. On the 28th April, the Tyldesley Rugby Club played the Lancashire Select Team in aid of the widow and family of the late James Quinn. The widow would have received a handsome amount, as the spectators amounted to over two thousand. Tyldesley won fourteen points to eleven.

Leigh Police Sports on the Athletic Ground, August 1925.

Supt. Whitehead presenting the Bedford Church team with the schoolboys' relay race shield at the Leigh Police Sports August 1925. In the rear: Inspector R.Stephenson, secretary and clerk of the course, and the teacher in charge of the winning team.

Leigh Harriers & Athletic Club

SEASON ENDING FEBRUARY 28th, 1923.

STATEMENT OF INCOME AND EXPENDITURE.

BAR ACCOUNT.

	£	s.	d.		£	s.	d.
February 28th, 1922, Stock	53	16	0	February 28th, 1923, Stock	42	18	1
Goods Cost	1195	18	2½	Cash Drawn	1502	8	5
Gross Profit	295	12	3½				
(Less Excise Duty £13 15 6)							
	£1545	6	6		£1545	6	6

INCOME	£	s.	d.	EXPENDITURE	£	s.	d.
To Subscriptions	56	14	0	By Owing to Treasurer Feb. 28th, 1922	0	14	7
,, Cash drawn in Bar	1502	8	5	,, Goods for Bar	1224	7	2½
,, Profit on Annual Sports	1	7	1	,, Excise Duty	13	15	6
,, Profit on Whist Drive and Dance	1	8	2	,, Harriers' Section	55	4	8
,, Profit on Christmas Draw	10	4	8	,, Makerfield Harriers' loss on Joint Sports	3	1	0
,, Harriers' Income—Gates, Entry Fees,				,, Social Evenings, etc.	6	17	10
Subscriptions to Prizes, etc.	8	14	8	,, Playing Cards	2	12	0
,, Socials	3	12	6	,, Football Jerseys, Entry Fee, Washing	4	1	0
,, Members' Whist Drives	3	11	10	,, Newspapers	3	6	6
,, Games	2	13	0	,, Games in Club	1	0	0
,, Sale of Football Jerseys	2	9	0	,, Printing and Posting	11	14	2½
,, Hire of Ground	60	11	0	,, Upkeep of ground, dressing rooms, etc.	30	0	2
,, Hire of Ground, Police Sports	25	0	0	,, Carting cinders for banking ground,			
,, Sale of Keys	0	16	0	tracks, etc.	13	15	7
,, Sale of Tax Tickets	34	4	4½	,, Alterations to Club Room	39	17	11
,, Bank Interest	0	6	7	,, Heating Apparatus	16	1	9
,, Subscriptions, etc., to New Pavilion	6	11	0	,, Coal, Oil and Cleaning Materials	12	5	5
,, Loans	57	0	0	,, Rent, Rates and Taxes	33	12	3
				,, Fire Insurance & Workmen's			
				Compensation Insurance	4	9	3
				,, Club Room Furniture, Glasses, etc.	4	14	4
				,, Donations, Delegations, etc.	4	12	3
				,, Purchase of Tax Tickets	25	4	3
				,, Bank Charges	2	3	0
				,, Wages and Insurance	197	15	8
				,, New Pavilion	54	16	8½
				,, Cash in Bank	2	5	8
				,, Treasurer's Cash in hand	4	5	6
				,, Harriers' Secretary's Cash in hand	4	18	1
	£1777	12	3½		£1777	12	3½

BALANCE SHEET.

LIABILITIES	£	s.	d.	ASSETS	£	s.	d.
To R. Green & Co.	65	11	8	By Stock in Bar	42	18	1
,, G. Shaw & Co.	5	4	6	,, Leigh Wednesday F.C.	6	0	0
,, Green & Leach	13	6	0	,, Makerfield Harriers	3	1	0
,, Burtonwood Brewery	15	8	0	,, Tax Tickets in hand	2	19	6½
,, J. Westwell	3	11	6	,, Deposit Leigh Corporation	5	0	0
,, Loan Money	57	0	0	,, Cash in Bank	2	5	8
				,, Cash in hand (Treasurer)	4	5	6
				,, Cash in hand (Harriers' Secretary)	4	18	1
				,, Adverse Balance	88	13	9½
	£160	1	8		£160	1	8

	£	s.	d.	
Adverse Balance	88	13	9½	
Adverse Balance Feb. 28th, 1922	56	16	2	March 25th, 1923.
Loss on Season £31 17 7½				JAMES HILTON ⎱
				WILLIAM SHARPE ⎰ *Auditors.*

W. H. Stafford & Co., Limited, Printers, 92 Railway Road, Leigh.

The Harriers Club accounts for 1923

The football section of the athletic club's accounts (Leigh Wednesday), shows the expenditure for jerseys, entry fees and laundry £14.1s, and income from the sale of jerseys at £2.9s.

The athletic club had a football section with the team name Leigh Wednesday A.F.C., which trained and played its home games on the athletic ground during the 1920s and 30s. The team had a remarkable 1929-30 season, winning the Wednesday League Championship and had the distinction of winning 17 consecutive matches.

Leigh Wednesday A.F.C. pictured outside the Harriers' club house, Jan 1927.

Back row:	Mr G.A.Wilson, Mr P.Sofe, B.Burton, H.Whittle, T.Lawless
	Mr L.Colling (Secretary)
Second row:	A.Such, J.Ritson, F.Bandy, Mr W.Ashton
Front row:	Mr P.Patterson, J.Fowler, O.Banner, T.Jones (Captain), J.Horrocks, W.Sanderson,
	Mr P.Gorman (Treasurer).

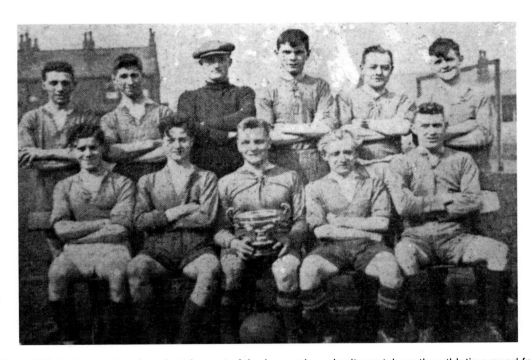

In May 1930 the team played against the rest of the league in a charity match on the athletic ground for the Leigh Infirmary fund. Councillor W.Hindley J.P. kicked off the game; Wednesday lost the match 4-1. After the match Councillor Hindley congratulated the teams and presented Leigh Wednesday with the Wednesday League championship cup, as pictured above.

Back row: Albert E.Sherrington, W.Baines, H.Whittle, J.Tatum, H.Newall, T.Woodcock
Front row: J.Bond, Alf.Sherrington, A.McLeod (Captain), J.H.Barnott, C.H.Perkins.

Leigh Harriers Sports, Half Mile Open Handicap, 26th May 1928.
The photo shows Tommy W.Gorse of Leigh running in second, on the bend.

Unfortunately for the success of the event, rain completely spoilt the annual sports promoted by the Leigh Harriers' officials. They faced a heavy loss, for there were not more than 1,500 spectators present at the most, and only a total of 500 entries. It was intended to run a 20-mile marathon race in preparation for a big event, which was the Manchester Marathon the following week but, owing to the weather, this was curtailed to 12-miles. Arthur Farrimond of Leigh Harriers beat Bryant and Norton of Bolton by only a few yards, in a time of 77 minutes.

70yds Handicap, for boys attending Leigh Elementary Day Schools, 26th May 1923
Winner- V.Hayman, 2nd J.Whittle, 3rd J.Ogden, followed by J.Jones, T.Smith and J.Smith.

Leigh Police Sports, 100yds race, (open to all Police) 18th August 1923

There were over 1,000 entrants for the 34 events, the spectators were treated to five hours of keenly contested races and wrestling matches. Due to alterations to the ground, cycling events were dispensed with, the track was not deemed suitable. During the afternoon, over a dozen pieces of music were played by the Glazebury Prize Band.

Following custom the meeting started with the 80yds young daughters of member's race,
18th August 1923.
Winner, J.Whittingham, 2nd E.Dixon, 3rd E.Lyon, 4th M.F.Cooper, who failed to gain a prize, was awarded a box of chocolates by the Mayor of Leigh, Councillor W.Collier.

Leigh Police Sports, August 1924.

Leigh Harrier Ellis Green, seen in the above picture winning the 100yds open handicap sprint final, on the athletic ground, in front of an 8,000 spectator crowd.

He also won the 220yds open handicap off the ten yard mark from his team mate Eddie Roberts, in a time of 22.4 sec, and eliminated the Olympic sprinter Walter Rangeley in one of the earlier heats of the 220yds.

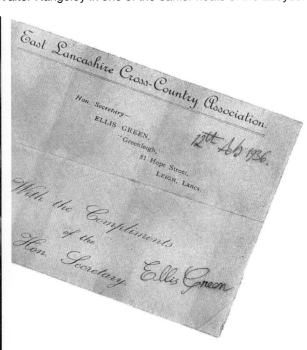

Ellis Green (1902-1987), pictured above in his Leigh mayoral robes, was the sprint champion during the 1920's for the Leigh Club. He was encouraged into the sport in 1916 by his uncle, James Edward Blears (1882-1966), who himself was a great sportsman, he played rugby centre forward for the Tyldesley, Wigan, Swindon and Lancashire Teams 1897-1916 and was also water-polo 'goalkeeper' for Tyldesley and a long distance walker.

Ellis became Hon. Asst. Secretary for the Athletic Club in 1923, and the Harriers section Secretary in 1924. In the 1930s he became a member of the Salford Harriers and Secretary of the Northern Cross Country Association 1935-1937. He was Hon. Secretary of the East Lancashire C.C.A. 1925-1939, and President in 1935. He acted as air raid warden in Leigh during the Second World War and in the 1940s he became secretary and then President of the Leigh Rugby Supporters Club. Green had been a Conservative member for St Thomas's ward since 1941, and was elected Mayor of Leigh in May 1952; he was the first tory Mayor for 15 years.

Results sheets from the Northern and East Lancashire cross country championships: 1925, 1926, 1928, and 1929, which now form part of the Harrier's large collection of programmes and results.

Harriers Club House Destroyed by Fire

Tragedy happened on the weekend that the lads won the senior East Lancashire cross country championships. One of the biggest fires which had occurred in Leigh for some time was discovered just before 6.30am on the morning of the 14th February 1927. The club's pavilion and recreation rooms on the athletic ground were found in flames; the Leigh Fire Brigade were soon on the scene, with Superintendent Annan in charge. An ample supply of water was available from a street hydrant and the Atherton brook (was also known as the Avenue brook), which ran just behind the club premises. The flames however, had got too fine a hold and, in spite of the efforts of the fire brigade, the whole of the recreation room, which consisted of two large First World War P.O.W. huts from 1919, arranged in the form of a letter L, were burnt out. The flames created a glare in the sky which was visible for miles around, and people going to their work were attracted in large numbers.

The piano, a billiard table, all the furniture, and practically all the contents of the bar were destroyed. The damage was estimated at £2,000, of which only £800 was covered by insurance. Only the wooden grandstand was saved from the flames. The outbreak was thought to have been caused by the flue of the heating apparatus overheating.

After The Fire

Though the buildings were insured, reconstruction would be costly and the club had to go into debt to re-build and re-equip the premises. Meanwhile, two garages joined together on the field sufficed as a bar and kept the members together. Eventually, in the summer of 1928, two more billets were brought from the old P.O.W. camp site in Etherstone Street, and erected on the athletic ground for a total of £50.00. They stood on the athletic ground until they were demolished in 1984, and were replaced by a new brick club house and buildings.

LEIGH HARRIERS AND ATHLETIC CLUB.

STATEMENT OF INCOME AND EXPENDITURE, Year ending February 28, 1927

INCOME.	£	s.	d.
March 1st, 1926—Cash in Bank ...	3	6	6
To Bar receipts	1660	12	1½
„ Billiard Table	29	3	0
„ Subscriptions	44	13	9
„ Ground	29	11	4
„ Games	4	1	6
„ Insurance rebate—Royal Insurance Co.	0	8	0
„ Fire Insurance Claim ...	794	10	0
„ Loan of Crockery, Cutlery, etc. ...	7	2	6
„ January Whist Drive and Dance—profit	13	5	9
„ Fire Salvage	4	5	8½
„ Bank Interest	0	11	0
„ Whist Drive receipts	608	12	0
	£3,200	**3**	**2**

EXPENDITURE.	£	s.	d.
By Amount owing to Treasurer ...	0	15	6½
„ Bar Goods	1223	18	5
„ Steward's wages and Insurance ...	194	13	0
„ Sports, Bars and Refreshment Rooms	11	5	6
„ Excise Duty	13	1	0
„ Grant to Gen. Sec. (2 years—to Feb. 28, 1927)	10	0	0
„ Subscriptions (50% to Harriers Section) ...	22	6	10
„ Grants, etc. ditto	89	10	11
„ Registration Fees, Licenses, Catering Rights	7	11	0
„ Rent, Rates and Taxes	20	3	6
„ Fire and Compensation Insurance ...	7	14	9
„ Gas, Water and Electricity ...	30	0	11
„ Stamps and Stationery, etc. ...	12	5	1½
„ Billiard Table Repairs (outs) ...	4	17	0
„ Newspapers	4	13	3
„ Playing Cards, etc.	2	15	0
„ Glasses, Bar Utensils and Repairs ...	7	1	11
„ Crockery, Cutlery, etc.	4	7	3
„ Sundry Payments	3	14	6
„ Printing and Advertising ...	5	14	0
„ Repairs, Renewals, Allowances (premises) ..	39	16	5½
„ Electric Light Alterations	4	14	9
„ Furniture, Curtains, Lino., etc. ...	29	10	1
„ Cleaning Materials	2	19	2
„ Painting and Decorating Allowance ...	8	17	11
„ Heating	15	3	8½
„ Ground Work and Allowance ...	29	10	0
„ Weed-killer	4	2	6
„ General Carting, Cinders and Allowances	25	7	2½
„ New Bridge	14	9	3
„ Sports, Bar and Timber	16	8	3
„ Billiards and Games	1	17	6
„ Free Meals	8	14	9½
„ Temporary premises	20	0	0
„ Salvage Work and Insurance ...	10	1	6
„ Donations, Delegations	5	19	6
„ Bank Commission and Cheque Books ...	3	11	0
„ Whist Drive Payments	566	2	10
„ Cash in hand 19 18 9			
„ Cash in Bank 696 8 7	716	7	4
	£3,200	**3**	**2**

BAR TRADING ACCOUNT.

Feb. 28th, 1926	£	s.	d.
Stock	62	9	2
Goods paid for	1223	18	5
Goods owing for	149	1	11
Excise duty	13	1	0
Profit (estimated)	441	18	7
	£1,890	**9**	**1**

Feb. 28, 1927	£	s.	d.
Stock	82	1	0½
Cash drawn	1660	12	1½
Cash allowed for Fire damage—Stock	44	10	0
Feb. 28, 1927			
Goods owing for	103	5	11
	£1,890	**9**	**1**

BALANCE SHEET.

ASSETS.	£	s.	d.
Cash in Bank...	696	8	7
Cash in hand	19	18	9
Bar Stock	82	1	0
Ground Hire	6	0	0
Tax Tickets	3	16	3
Deposit with Leigh Corporation ...	5	0	0
	£813	**4**	**7**

LIABILITIES.	£	s.	d.
Bar Goods	149	1	11
New Bridge Materials	10	15	4
Timber for Fencing and Alterations ...	8	15	2
Balance—Assets over Liabilities ...	644	12	2
	£813	**4**	**7**

Audited and found correct, March 23rd, 1927,

JAMES E. SUMNER   } Auditors.
S. HARE

By March 1927, the insurance claim had been paid into the club accounts and provided the committee with sufficient funds to purchase the materials to rebuild a new club house. The club bought two garages at a cost of £20.00, for the use as temporary facilities on the field until the new premises were completed. The club also managed to purchase a new bridge to cross the Atherton brook leading from Charles Street on to the athletic ground. This was required as the existing one was over 40 years old and had fallen into a state of disrepair.

Leigh Police Sports, 18ᵗʰ August, 1928.
Prizes valued at over £180 were a splendid inducement to the competitors.
The officials in the photo left to right are: Inspector R.Stephenson who was secretary and clerk of the course,
Mr J.Isherwood, acting steward, Mr Fred Brooks, jeweller of Railway Road, who supplied the prizes,
Superintendent Johnson Vice-President and Inspector Atkinson, steward.

At the Police sports 18ᵗʰ August 1928, the Mayoress presented the winners gold medals to members of
Bedford Church schoolboys' relay 'A' team.
Left to right: F.Price (Captain) J.Page, T.Starkie, and L.Hardie,
Others on the photo are, from **Left to right:** The Mayor Mr Wm.Hindley, Mr A.Lee teacher in charge, the Vicar
of Bedford Church Rev.J.T.Lawton M.A, and Counc Wm.Collier J.P.

There were a large number of entries for the Leigh Harriers club sports in June 1928, but no competitors were keener than the sons of members. Photo shows J.B.Eckersley winning the 70yds boys' handicap, Jos Eckesley was 2nd, and T.Brown came in a good 3rd, all residents of Lowton. They were followed by W.Jackson, W.Boydell and F.Harrison.

The finish of the youth's 100yds race at Leigh Police Sports Aug 1929. C.Hampson of Astley ran a good second behind the Salford Harriers lad.

The picture above was taken in 1926, and shows Harry Bailey, Richard Sutton and Jacky Bond with Harriers trainer Fred Brown. Fred was a very good cross country runner in his time and competed well into his forties. He was in the junior team when they ran third in the East Lancs cross country championships in Manchester 1913, and was a founder member when the athletic club was reformed in September 1909. Fred was the Honorary Secretary for the Harriers section from 1927 until 1948, and became President of the Harriers Athletic club from 1955 to 1963.
The young boy in the centre is Jacky Bond who became the Lancs Youths Track Champion in 1927 at 880yds, and also ran third in the 440yds, he finished 2nd in the Northern Counties 440yds the same year.

The Harriers Medley Relay Track Team 1928
Harry Bailey,   Jimmy Andrews,   Teddy Roberts,   William Tom Battersby,   Unknown
440ys   880yds   220yds   220yds
Roberts and Battersby were two of the Harriers best sprinters during the 1920s and early 30s.

Leigh members in the club's billiard room, January 1929
On the far left is Fred Brown, Harriers secretary and trainer. Next to him, wearing a bow-tie and flat cap, is Ernest William Walton. The chap sitting at the billiard table wearing a flat cap is Billy Holt, the local road sweeper, and standing behind him is one of the local off duty policemen.

Leigh Harriers sports June 1929

The final of the 100yds youth handicap, W.W.Potts of Warrington, winning in a time of 9.85sec, in 2nd place Jason Frayne of Liverpool Harriers, 3rd was C.Virgin from Salford A.C. and 4th G.Brew of Liverpool.

Leigh Harriers held an athletic sports meeting on 14th June 1924, in aid of the Leigh Infirmary extension fund. The above caricature picture of the main officials appeared in the local newspaper that week.

The Leigh team were invited to run at Blackpool on 19th October 1929, in a 7-mile road race starting from Talbot Square, Blackpool. Alderman J.Potter, Mayor, acted as starter. H.R.Clarke was the pacemaker and led the sixty starters along the promenade.

Listed below are the top finishers in the race, all of whom are pictured above.

1st T.Evenson, Salford Harriers   6th H.Doggett, Salford Harriers
2nd G.W.Bailey, Salford Harriers   7th T.P.Campbell, Salford Harriers
3rd J.Crewdson, Blackpool & Fylde   8th J.Andrews, Leigh Harriers
4th R.Sutton, Leigh Harriers   9th E.J.Simms, Leigh Harriers
5th J.P.Cleary, Salford Harriers.

Bob Critchley and John Willy Grainey of Leigh were placed just outside the top ten.

Five mile race from Stanley Park, Blackpool, on Boxing Day 1929, for the J.R.Quayle Cup.

In the centre of the photograph is Harry R.Clarke of Leigh, a founder member of Blackpool & Fylde Harriers, which was approaching its first anniversary. Standing next to him is the new Mayor of Blackpool, George William Gath. The only Leigh representative was Arthur Farrimond, pictured standing next to the Mayoress in his 1924 Olympic marathon shirt. The Blackpool athletes in the picture are J.Crewdson who was the eventual winner, J.Davitt 2nd, W.C.Brayshaw 3rd, also J.O'Hara, J.Helm, J.Platt and H.R.Clarke. The officials also in the picture are: W.Maloney, H.Gregory, Mr James Yates M.B.E., Counc J.R.Quayle, J.Clarke and J.H.Hardwick of Salford Harriers.

Harry R.Clarke on the left and Arthur Farrimond on the right. Arthur trained with Harry to develop his running speed for his Olympic marathon bid. Their trainer Jack Clarke, Harry's brother, stands behind them, March 1924.

Private Arthur Farrimond, B.E.F.
Regt. No. 2774, 12th Platoon. C.coy.
9th Batt. Highlanders, The Royal Scots.
Pictured above December 1914.

Arthur Farrimond was born on 30th September 1893, to James and Margaret Farrimond, at 9 Hill Street, Hindley, Lancashire. He won his first race at the age of seventeen, at the Westhoughton town sports in 1910. He joined the Bolton Harriers club and, in 1911, joined Leigh Harriers. In February 1914 he became a medal winner in the junior East Lancashire cross country championships.
When the war broke out he was working as a commercial traveller for Messrs.J.Smith & Co., Wine and Spirit Merchants. He enlisted in the 9th Royal Scots on November 11th 1914, and whilst serving in France he won the French Medallion in a one and a half mile race for his regiment. He reached the front line in January 1915, where he was wounded in the knee. He was again wounded in the stomach in August 1916, as a result of a bayonet charge, and made a full recovery whilst in Ward 16, of the Merry Flatts Hospital, Govan, Glasgow.

In March 1915, one of his letters home was published in the local newspaper, speaking of his ordeal in the trenches, and also saying he had made up his mind to try and get to Berlin in 1916 for the Olympic Games. Unknown to him, there would be no 1916 games and he would not resume his training until 1919, too late for even the 1920 games. Arthur's first race after the war was a 5-miler organised by Makerfield Harriers at Newton, 21st March 1919, it was the first athletic event of imprortance held in Lancashire since 1914, and was supported well by fifteen other clubs who turned out their finest athletes. Arthur beat the 1912 Olympian Walter Scott, who was running for his new club, Salford Harriers. Three weeks later on 12th April , Arthur raced again in an open invitation race at Leigh, over a 4-mile cross country course, starting at the Charles Street ground, twenty eight runners started, Arthur won by beating another 1912 Olympian, Edward Owen of Broughton Harriers into second place.

Arthur married Emily Birch in 1922, and he regained his running fitness after the war. He was becoming well known as a distance runner, but he still won shorter distance races, like the one-mile races at Abergele and Whitehaven. He ran second in the 1923 and 1924 Manchester Marathons, and it was from these races that he was selected to run the marathon for Britain at the 1924 Olympics in Paris.

Arthur was the second Britain to finish in Paris, and had to suffer the last few miles with a twist to his ankle, which he received trying to avoid a civilian who insisted on running alongside him. There were fifty eight entrants representing the other world countries in the race, and it was no small achievement to finish seventeenth in an Olympic marathon. Arthur returned home to his new job as an electrician in the employment of the Wigan Coal and Iron Company. He continued to run in races for the next fifty years with the Leigh Harriers club. In later years Arthur ran a newsagent's shop in Westhoughton and died in November 1978, aged 85. His ashes are in the family grave at Hindley Cemetery. His wife Emily died in 1984 aged 90; they had no children.

Arthur in his G.B. Olympic Vest, 1924.

The winners of the 1929 Rivington fell race, finished in order of line up.
Left to right: Winner -Thomas P.Campbell of Salford Harriers, George Wm.Bailey (Buxton), who later ran for Salford Harriers, Sam Dodd (Chester) Wirral Harriers and Arthur Farrimond of Leigh Harriers A.C.

Cross Country .East Lancs. Placings

1914	3rd	Junior
1921	4th	Senior
1922	7th	Senior
1923	3rd	Senior
1925	20th	Senior
1926	4th	Senior

Marathons

1923	2nd	Manchester Sporting Chronicle
1924	2nd	Manchester Sporting Chronicle
1924	17th	Paris Olympics
1924	5th	Manchester Sporting Chronicle four clubs carnival.
1925	4th	Manchester Sporting Chronicle
1927	8th	Manchester Sporting Chronicle
1928	16th	Manchester Sporting Chronicle

Other Major Races

1914, 4th junior northern cross country championship, Arthur won a gold medal for the first man home in an unplaced team.
1925 4th Northern Counties senior 10-mile track championship.
1929 4th in the Rivington fell race

The commemorative participation bronze medal Arthur received on 13th July 1924, at the Paris Olympics where he finished 17th in the marathon.

Major Races

1924   2nd   Northern Cross Country Champs
1924   11th   National Cross Country Champs
1924   9th   England International
1924   2nd   Northern Counties 10- Mile track
1931   4th   Northern Counties 10- Mile track
1931   10th   Northern Cross Country Champs

East Lancs. Cross Country

1922   4th   Junior
1923   1st   Junior
1924   2nd   Senior
1925   10th   Senior
1928   6th   Senior
1931   5th   Senior

Marathons

1931   2nd   Sutton-in-Ashfield, 20-miles
1931   3rd   Polytechnic, Windsor to Stamford
           Bridge,   2hrs 45min 55sec
1931   3rd   A.A.A.   2hrs 54min 06sec
1931   3rd   Blackpool,   2hrs 47min 43sec

Harry R.Clarke in 1922, with his prizes and trophies,
including the Harry Brown Shield won for the clubs 1,000yds championship.

Henry Richard Clarke who liked to be known as Harry, was born to George and Annie Clarke on 30th December 1899, at Flapper Fold, Atherton, Lancashire. As a junior he joined Bolton United Harriers, and in November 1920 he ran in an inter-club race over seven miles at Farnworth, he came third behind Eddie Kenrick and George C.L.Wallach.
In 1921 he and his brother Jack joined the Salford Harriers club and had some success as members of their cross country team. Later that season they both joined Leigh Harriers where Jack began training Harry; his main training partner was Arthur Farrimond, from Hindley.
In 1922 he entered the junior East Lancs cross country championships at the Manchester racecourse and ran fourth, the following year he won the title with ease. 1924 proved to be a brilliant year for Harry, he became a senior and ran eleventh in the National, and thus earned himself an England international jersey. He ran for England at Gosforth Park, Newcastle-on-Tyne, in March 1924, where he ran in ninth position, helping England to beat five other countries to win the international. He also won the Liverpool 4-mile handicap from the 45 second mark, and ran second to Sewall in the N.C.A.A. ten miles; he only lost the race by eighteen seconds.
In the 1924 senior East Lancs and the Northern cross country championships he ran second. Six years later he entered the Blackpool marathon and looked an easy winner until he had to give up in the last mile through leg trouble, Harold Wood won the race. The following year Harry ran third in the same race, he also ran third in the A.A.A. marathon and third in the Polytechnic marathon from Windsor to Stamford Bridge. All three races were run in the space of three weeks, which was a marvellous performance. In late 1928 he became one of the founder members of the Blackpool & Fylde Harriers club. In the autumn of 1931, he officially left Leigh Harriers and went to live permanently in Blackpool where he ran a business. Harry died in May 1961; he left a wife, two sons and a daughter.

Harry 'No 29' with the English cross country team at Gosforth Park, Newcastle-upon-Tyne, before their International match, 22nd March 1924.
Left to right standing: F.J.Wright - trainer, H.Newbould - President N.C.C.U., 1920 & 21,
C.Otway - life member of the N.C.C.U, R.Stanton, C.E.Blewitt, W.T.Rainbow - President of the International Board, J.E.Webster, unknown.
Left to right sitting: H.R.Clarke, J.C.Benham, A.N.Sewell, E.Harper, J.Williams, W.M.Cotterell.

The members of the newly formed Blackpool & Fylde Harriers Club, pictured in February 1929.
John Crewdson is standing second from the left with Harry R.Clarke. Harry's brother Jack is standing behind them, wearing a flat cap.

Geoffrey Turner winning the high-jump on Leigh Athletic ground, August 1931

Geoffrey Turner was born on the 16th May in 1907 to Alfred and Emily S.Turner at 58 Bond Street, Leigh, christened, Ignatius Geoffrey Barker Turner.
His father had his own plumbing business on Chapel Street facing St Thomas's Church, and had a house built on Green Lane, Leigh, which he named Woodlawn; the family moved there in 1909. Geoffrey, their only son was educated at Hawksyard College, near Litchfield, Staffordshire, and for several years he was employed at the local Pennington Mill Co. Ltd., with a view to entering the cotton manufacturing business where his mother was a director and had been since 1924. However, for some time he had also been studying scientific farming and it was his intention to take over a large farm at Stretton, Cheshire.
Geoffrey established a reputation as a high-jumper and hurdles competitor and was a member of both the Earlestown and Leigh Athletic clubs. He got started in athletics by casually visiting the grounds of the Earlestown Athletic Club, where he saw a group of men high-jumping. They had scaled a certain height and were surprised when young Turner declared that he could clear the same height in ordinary attire, which he did, and he was subsequently persuaded to commence training.

Geoffrey, standing 6'3½ " and weighing 12st 8lbs, had his first high jump competition in 1926, at a C.Y.M.S. meeting in Liverpool, where he only jumped 5' 1". Undaunted however, he entered for the Northern Counties championships three weeks later, and there he increased his high-jump by seven inches and came second. The following year, Geoffrey began training with ex-Sergeant Major Miller, who was an army high-jump champion, with his guidance Geoffrey won the 1927 Northern Counties high-jump championship, with a leap of 5' 11".

Lancashire Champion	1926, 28, 29, 31
Northern Champion	1927, 28, 29, 30, 31.
Northern 100yds Hurdles Champion	1929
A.A.A. Championships equal second	1930
British Empire games - 6th	1930

Geoffrey represented his country seven times, and competed at the Amsterdam Olympics in 1928, where he was unplaced. In 1929 he jumped 1.94m = 6'4½ ", at Burnley. This took Turner to the top of the 1929 European high-jump rankings and to equal fifth in the world. The same year he equalled the British record with a leap of 6ft 5ins, at Widnes, but there were no qualified officials at the meeting so the record could not stand. His last public appearance was in August 1931, at the Earlestown ground with an exhibition jump.

In March 1932, just after he had purchased Fir Tree Farm, Stretton, Cheshire, for the sum of £3,200, he was taken ill with septic tonsils. He was attended by Dr Alistair McCloud of Leigh, and later three specialists, two from Manchester and one from London. A blood transfusion from a young man of twenty four was tried but, despite every effort to preserve his life, the case proved hopeless and he died of septicaemia at his parents' house, 2nd May 1932, aged twenty four, nine weeks after being diagnosed. He died a few months before he was due to go to the Los Angeles Olympics, his death was made even more tragic by the fact that his Wedding Day was only four weeks away. His fiancée, Miss Nora Spelman, of Earlestown said he had a very happy, generous and likeable personality, and he had friends in many quarters. Nora eventually inherited Woodlawn and never married, she died in April 1981, aged 81.

Geoffrey's funeral was held in St Joseph's Church, and he was buried at Leigh Cemetery. Friends, family. Messrs. J.Wightman and L.Allwood of Earlestown Viaduct Athletic Club, J.Dickinson and F.Brown of Leigh Harriers Athletic Club were present.

The picture on the left shows G.Turner congratulating the young sixteen year old Northern Counties A.A. women's high jump champion, Miss Dorothy Manley of Atherton, who competed for the Bolton United Harriers club on the Leigh athletic ground, August 1931. Dorothy was the daughter of Sergeant Manley of the Atherton Fire Brigade.

On the above right G.Turner is pictured in1931 with his new trainer Mr Patrick 'Paddy' Duffy, who lived at Bedford Square, Leigh. Paddy worked as a colliery driller up until 1940, then at R.O.F. Risley. He was also trainer to Leigh R.F.C., the Police and several local athletes. In his early years between 1907 and 1914 he won many of sprint handicaps around the Leigh area, winning stakes of cash prizes up to £60. He died in July 1952 aged 63.

Geoffrey Turner winning the high-jump handicap off scratch, in front of 6,000 spectators, after a final jump-off with W.Roberts of Salford. Geoffrey won with a clearance of 6'½"=1.84m, at the 34th Bury Police annual sports, 17th June 1928, at Gigg Lane football field, Bury.

Geoffrey Turner the Leigh high-jumper, who competed in the 1928 Olympic Games in Amsterdam. Harry Ratcliffe followed Ike Taylor as the Turner's family chauffer. Harry and Geoffrey are pictured above with their shooting guns and ferrets in 1928.

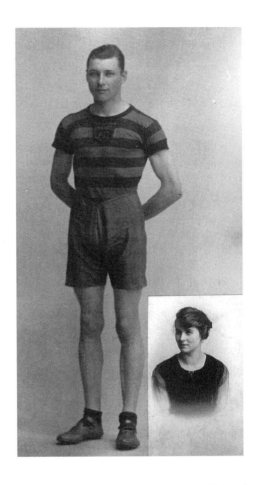

The picture on the left, taken in 1927, shows Geoffrey in his Earlestown Viaduct A.C. colours. Geoffrey's fiancée Nora Spelman (inset), christend Hannah, at Newton-le-Willows, May 1899.

The picture on the right shows Geoffrey's first high-jump competition, at a C.Y.M.S meeting at Broad Green, Liverpool on 24th May 1926, only clearing 5'1". Three weeks later in the Northern Counties Championships at Wath-upon-Dearne, South Yorks., he improved to 5'8" = 1.73m.

Geoffrey Turner's commemorative participation bronze medal, which he received at the Amsterdam Olympic Games 29th July 1928. Also his 46 page official handbook, published by the Olympic committee.

Richard Sutton International Athlete 1929

Richard (Dick) Sutton was born in May 1899 and from an early age his father tried to make a runner out of him but gave it up as useless. Even whilst he was in the Navy during the 1914-18 World War he did not so much as enter the events on sport days. His first job on leaving school in 1911, aged twelve years old, was delivering newspapers along Nel Pan Lane, he picked them up from the Leigh Railway Station, and carried them over a mile to Westleigh, sometimes he worked up to eight hours a day. Dick said later in life that that's probably how he acquired strong arms and legs. In 1912, he worked for three months at the Spindle Works, after which he was employed by Hayes Spinning Company, where he worked in the spinning room, after a dispute with his bosses he left the factory and started at the Wigan Coal and Iron Company (Priestners Pit) as a haulage hand.

In May 1918, towards the end of the First World War Dick joined the Navy because of a letter he had received from his brother Joe, who was serving in the trenches. His brother wrote about the harsh conditions and horrors of war at the front, and suggested that Dick enlist in the Navy, before he was called up for Army duty, suggesting that at least he would have a dry bed to fight from. Dick trained in the R.N.V.R. at Crystal Palace, Norwood, London, then at Davenport, where he passed out as a Signaller. He was then transferred to H.M.S. Tay at Plymouth. After being demobed in May 1919, he returned to Priestners Pit where he trained with future career prospects as a Manager. Jobs undertaken were ripping, cockering, heading-cutters, long wall cutters, drilling etc. he was working as shot lighter at the time he met Fred Brown the Harriers' trainer with whom he was working, Fred persuaded Dick to start cross country running and in less than four months of training he had won the Leigh Harriers senior long distance cross country championship, which was then a distance of seven miles.

In June 1923, he married Mary Cox at St Joseph's Church, Leigh. The following month, when he was running a 440yds hurdle race at the Bolton Sports, he collided with another runner while going over the barrier, he fell and caught the back of his head on the hurdle, and was taken to Bolton Royal Hospital with amnesia, which lasted for twelve months; he could never remember his wedding day for the rest of his life.

During the 1920's and 30's he made running his chief hobby, and well over £200 of prizes have fallen to his credit, the chief races being the obstacle races, half-mile, one and two-mile flat races and in the winter he also ran the cross country with great success. Dick won numerous handicaps, among them the Leigh Harriers 7-mile Christmas handicap off scratch mark giving starts of up to seven minutes on three occasions. He was the first man home in a great number of cross country inter-club races against the Bolton and Horwich clubs.

In 1925 he started working for Pilkington Collieries, Astley Pit, which later became known as Manchester Collieries, and in 1928 he passed his overseers papers and became a colliery fireman. After the 1936 explosion at Astley Green Colliery his health deteriorated and in 1940 he retired from his job because of a severe breakdown in health, he had already given up racing a few years before. In May 1940 he was under doctor's orders to work in the open air, so he began window cleaning and working as a freelance photographer, covering civic meetings, weddings and sports etc. for the local papers.

Dick's other interest, and hobby for most of his life, was photography, working part-time for the local newspapers, he became a well known photographer and his subjects were varied. He joined the Leigh Literary Society photographic section in its early days and acted as its secretary for many years. He was a constant prize winner; in 1948 he won the Bronze Plaque of the Lancashire and Cheshire Photographic Union and remained on their list of lecturers until the last few years of his life, when travelling became too onerous. He was a founder member of the Atherton Photographic Society and up to his death he was a member of the Leigh Camera Club. For several terms he taught photography at Tyldesley Adult Education centre and also became a member of the Lancashire Photographic Society and acted as its Leigh Treasurer.

In 1942 and up to his retirement in 1964, he became a school caretaker, first at Leigh Boys Grammar School, then at St Joseph's School, ending his working life at the Hope Carr Nursery School in Mather Lane. After retirement he took a keen interest in bowling and was a well known figure around Butts Park Bowling Green. Mr and Mrs Sutton celebrated their Golden Wedding Anniversary in June 1973; he died the same year, at his home in Hooten Lane, Leigh, aged 74 on Tuesday 18th September. A requiem mass was held at St Joseph's Church, followed by cremation at Overdale, Bolton. He left a wife and one daughter, whose permission was given for her father's sporting photographic material to be published in this book.

Senior East-Lancashire
cross county championship
gold medal, 1929

Leigh Harriers 1,000yds
track championship
gold medal, 1924

Manchester Business
Houses
cross country championship
gold medal, 1930

Start of the senior East Lancashire cross country championship, 4th Feb 1928, at Lower Pools, Heaton, Bolton. The winner was Teddy Rawlinson of Leigh from Abel Ward of Bury and J.Melling of Middleton Harriers. Leigh won the team race followed by: Middleton, Bury, Bolton and then Royton.

Leigh Harriers juniors won the St Helens & District cross country championships at Newton-le-Willows, January 1934, the Sutton Harriers team ran second.

Left to right, back row: Harry Brown 3rd, Jack Isherwood, Sid Peters, L.Gerrard, Austin Littler 10th.
Front row: Jimmy Unsworth 2nd, Billy Rose, Jimmy Noon 17th, Tommy Mort 8th, Arthur Dickinson 16th.

**Eddie J.Simms, pictured above on the
Leigh Harriers Athletic track in 1932.**

**Eddie and his son Arnold, pictured with his
silver prizes and trophies in 1947.**

Eddie J.Simms was born 23rd Janurary 1906 at Barrow-in-Furness, Cumbria to Edward and Elizabeth Simms.
He was the club's 10-mile track champion in 1934-36 and after the war in 1946-48. In 1949 he was only just
beaten to the line by his club team mate Fred Norris, who later ran for Bolton United Harriers and represented
Great Britain at the 1952 and 1956 Olympic Games.
Teddy, as he was known to his friends, held the club's 10-mile track record at 54min 12sec and his record
stood for 40 years, until Kenny Peers beat his record in the 1970s.
The last time Teddy won the Leigh Harriers 10-mile track championship was in 1953 and he still holds
the over-40's veteran club record for the event, which he set in 1948 at 57min 11sec.

There have been many dedicated members over the last one hundred years or so at the Harriers Athletic Club,
Teddy himself was one of them. His efforts have always been noted and appreciated at the club. After his
day's work in the local coal mine, he would complete his athletic training then carry out some ground work on
the track, or paper work in the club house. He was the team captain of the Harriers in the 1940s and 50s, and
he was the Harriers General Secretary 1957-58.
His family and friends understood his love and dedication to the club as he had spent most of his life being an
active member of the Leigh Harriers Athletic and Social club. Sadly, Teddy passed away in 1988, aged 82.
Teddy was one of those athletes who was dedicated to his sport and to club activities; his achievements were
numerous.

    1931- Northern Counties 10-mile track championship, 5th
    1934- East Lancs, Cross Country, 4th
    1934- St Helens and District Championships 2nd place, 1st team
    1935- Manchester Business Houses Shield, Astley Pit, 1st team
    1946- East Lancs, Cross Country, 5th
    1948- East Lancs, Cross Country, 3rd

    1933- Manchester Daily Dispatch Marathon 3rd
    1934- Manchester Daily Dispatch Marathon 5th
    1934- Blackpool Marathon 6th
    1935- Blackpool Marathon 5th
    1936- Blackpool Marathon 6th

Eddie J.Simms, Jimmy Unsworth and Billy Rose on the Leigh track in 1932

Start of one of the Harriers weekly club races 1933, only 6 names are known: Eddie J.Simms, Eddie Rawlinson, Wiliam Miles Simpson, John Willy Grainey, Jack Isherwood, Tommy Mort.

Leigh Harriers Junior and Senior teams 1929-30

From left to right
Back row :   3 unknowns, H.Cox, unknown, Bradbury, W.Worsley.
Third row: W.M.Simpson, unknown, J.Cheetham, F.Brown, J.W.Grainey, P.Bent, J.Waters,
                W.Andrews, J.Emerson, W.G.Simpson, unknown, unknown, W.Harrison,
                G.Turner, J.Dickinson, J.Clarke.
Second row: A.Farrimond, H.R.Clarke, B.Thomas, R.W.Kettle, H.Bailey, S.Bradbury, R.Sutton, M.Thorpe
Front row: S.Isherwood, J.Andrews, unknown, unknown, T.Briscoe, E.Rawlinson

Harriers on the Athletic Ground, 1933-34 cross country season
From left to right
Back row: W.G.Simpson, W.M.Simpson, J.Noon, B.Cartwright, Frank Brown, T.Briscoe,
               J.Andrews, Fred Brown.
Middle row: T.Taylor, I.Cartwright, unknown, N.Massey.
Front row: Unknown, E.Rawlinson, H.Whittle, E.J.Simms, unknown.

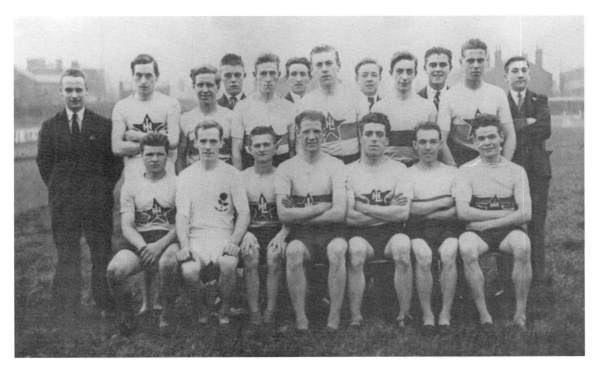

Harriers Group 1929-30 season pictured on the Charles Street athletic ground
Left to right
Back row: J.Bond, F.Dixon, H.Whittle, unknown, J.Andrews, Noon, W.G.Simpson, unknown, Gaskell, unknown, F.Brown, unknown.
Front row: S.Isherwood, R.Sutton, I.Cartwright, B.Banks, H.Cox, E.J.Simms, B.Critchley.

The Harriers Team pictured March 1935
Left to right
Back row: T.Abrams, S.Peters, J.B.Whitfield, unknown, A.Darwell, J.Andrews, T.Mort, unknown, J.Isherwood, unknown, N.Thomas, T.Green, F.Brown.
Middle row: A.J.Taylor, J.W.Grainey, H.Brown, J.Unsworth, R.Sutton, J.Cartwright, E.Cheetham.
Front row: W.Boydell, H.Smith, Bradbury, 3 unknowns, A.E.Simms, E.J.Simms, J.Noon, T.Cartwright, unknown, J.Such, J.Cheetham

The Harriers track championships held on Sat 30th Jan 1932. The photograph shows the three champions being awarded their medals by the club chairman Mr J.Hill in the concert room of the club house.
Left to right, Fred Brown - Harriers Secretary, William Harrison - Treasurer, John Dickinson-General Secretary, Harry Brown-youths 3-mile champion (17min 27sec), I.Cartwright- Junior 7-mile champion (40min 26sec), Richard Sutton-senior 10-mile champion (55min 05sec), Mr J.Hill-Chairman.

Leigh Harriers sprinters and middle distance runners on the athletic track 1934
Left to right: Arthur Darwell, Norman Thomas, unknown, Ted Roberts, Jimmy Andrews,
William Tom Battersby, Joe Cartwright, Tommy Cartwright, Jimmy Noon, unknown.

Leigh Harriers Club Committee Members, on the Athletic ground 1930.
Notice the Leigh Harrier's logo fob chains inside their jackets.

From left to right
Standing: W.Harrison, J.Aspinall, W.Worsley, W.M.Simpson, P.Bent, T.Collier, W.Boydell, J.Hill, F.Brown, J.Dickinson.
Sitting: R.Sutton, unknown, M.Thorpe, H.Smith, B.Thomas, J.Andrews.

Harriers cross country team and officials, photographed on the athletic ground, in January 1933

Back row left to right: I.Cartwright, B.Cartwright, E.Rawlinson, F.Gaskell, unknown, J.B.Whitfield, unknown, A.Amoss, 2 unknowns, H.Smith.
Third row: unknown, S.Peters, T.Green, T.E.Hudson, J.Clarke, J.Noon, G.Braizier, T.Mort, O.Hough, Frank Brown, R.Sutton, unknown, T.N.Massey, R.W.Kettle, J.Andrews, P.Bent, B.Thomas. J.Cheetham, J.Isherwood, T.Rose.
Second row: H.Hindley, E.J.Simms, S.H.Whittle, A.Dickinson, W.Harrison (treasurer), Fred Brown, J.L.Prescott (Mayor), J.Dickinson (secretary), H.Brown, J.W.Grainey, B.Rose.
Front row: J.Boydell, L.Gerrard, unknown, J.Unsworth, B.White, unknown.

The Mayor and Mayoress, Councillor and Mrs T.Hindley, presenting prizes to the first three in the final of the ladies 100yds sprint handicap flat race at the Harriers open sports,
Miss F.Humphries of Salford Harriers won the first prize from Miss D.Williams of Manchester A.C. and O.Moores of Manchester Harriers.
In the 3,000 spectator crowd was Mr J.J.Tinker M.P., who enjoyed watching the 10stone division wrestling match. The final bout was between W.Jefferies of Leigh Harriers and his club mate
Robert Owen, Jeffries beat Owen on a points decision. The proceeds of the sports, held on
28th May 1932, were in aid of the local Infirmary fund,

Leigh Open Sports, 19th August 1932.
Competitors in the first heat of the 880yds open handicap, rounding the bend on the last lap. Leading on the inside lane is Tommy S.Dixon, the 440 and 880yds Lancashire champion from Hindley.

An inter-club run from the Victoria Hotel, Horwich, 18th Nov 1933, between the Leigh, Bolton and Horwich teams. The Leigh team is pictured on the left, Horwich is in the centre and Bolton is on the far right of the photograph.

Above is the Harriers' fixtures and results book from the 1930s, belonging to the Leigh Harriers team captain, Dick Sutton. It is pictured open at the page dated 18th Nov 1933, which shows the results of the inter-club run between Leigh, Bolton and Horwich.

Leigh Harriers sports, 19th August, 1933.

On the left of the photo is John Dickinson, General Secretary of the Athletic Club, the person in the centre ready to present the silver cup is unknown. On the right is Mr Fred Brown who was the Harriers Hon. Secretary and treasurer at that time.

Beautiful weather had favoured the day's open sports with over 3,000 in attendance and 650 entries, including many well known competitors. There were four championship events being decided during the afternoon. The Lancashire county youths 880yds winner was Austin Littler of Leigh Harriers, the Lancashire county bantamweight wrestling winner was Joe Reid, the senior 440yds Lancs county championship was won by Walter Rangeley of the Salford Athletic Club, and the Northern Cycling Union 440yds championship was won by Mr W.Gorton of Manchester Athletic Club they were watched by the Mayor and Mayoress, Councillor and Mrs J.L.Prescott, and Mr J.J.Tinker.M.P.

The only known photograph of the old steeplechase water-jump on the Charles Street ground, showing someone attempting to clear the jump but landing very awkwardly, a member of the St John Ambulance Brigade is on hand just in case! August 1933.

Austin Littler, photographed before winning the Lancashire junior 880yds championship at the Leigh Harriers track sports,19th August 1933.

Austin was born 28th August 1915, and lived at Windlehust Avenue, St Helens. He competed for Leigh Harriers in the early 1930s, his coach Jim Gornall of Duke Street trained him well, he won the Junior Lancs county 880yds and 1-mile championships in 1933, along with the northern 440yds.
In 1934 he won the Harriers Track 1,000yds shield, the youngest to do so, and also won the A.A.A. Junior 1-mile. Later that year he joined the St Helens club Pilkington Recreational Harriers, and went on to become one of the U.K. top 880yds runners and represented his country. He achieved a best time of 1min 51.4sec for the 880yds.

Leigh Club Championship Wins

1933	440yds	Northern Junior	57.8 sec
1933	880yds	Lancs. Junior	2min 05.2 sec
1933	1-mile	Lancs Junior	4min 50.1 sec
1934	880yds	Northern Junior	2min 04.6 sec
1934	1-mile	Northern Junior	4min 43.6 sec
1934	1-mile	A.A.A. Junior	4min 39.0 sec
1934	St Helens & District C.C. Champs Team		

Saturday, 19th August 1933, Leigh Harriers Track Sports
Left to right: Mr Joe J.Tinker M.P., Mayor James Langley Prescott, Major Cross, Mr and Mrs Tillotson of the Leigh Journal and crouched down in front of the 3,000 crowd is Tom Burke the world famous tenor singer, known as the Lancashire Caruso.
Thomas Aspinall Burke born 2nd March1890, began to show his singing talents in the children's operettas whilst performing with the St Joseph's R.C.church players where he later joined the choir. During the next thirty years he performed and sang in concerts all over the world. He helped out St Joseph's church with charity concerts whenever he made visits back to Leigh and held singing classes for vocally talented individuals of Leigh. Tom died 13th September 1969, and is buried at Wallington Cemetery, Surrey.

Dorothy Whittaker with the Harriers' winners shield. She won the first ever Leigh Harriers schoolgirl 80yds championship in July 1935, in a time of 10.25 sec. Her grandfather was Joe Brisco the Leigh sprint champion in the 1880s.

Leigh Harriers group after a training session on the Athletic Ground, Nov 1934.
The only names known are Norman Thomas, A.Amoss, Jack Isherwood, Tommy Mort,
John Willy Grainey, Eddie J.Simms and his son Arnold.

Leigh Harriers Open Sports, August 1934

Twenty year old Jack Lyon of Leigh Harriers is pictured centre, winning the 100yds sprint open race from J.A.Davidson of Manchester A.C. on the inside lane. Running in 3rd place is W.Kelly of Pilkington Recreational Harriers.

Jack also won the 220yds that afternoon; he was the Lancashire silver medallist for the 100yds, achieved in July 1934 at Irlam. The following year he became the 220yds Lancashire champion and held the Leigh Harriers club's 100yds title from 1934 to 1937.

In July 1938 he ran second in the Lancashire 100yds championships at Leigh and joined the Sefton Harriers club in the same year.

Jack Lyon of Rivington Avenue, St Helens, on the Leigh Harriers track,
he began to compete for the Leigh Harriers club during the 1930s.

Tommy at the Leigh track 1934-35 season.   **At his home, Blackmoor, Astley 1935.**

Tommy Cartwright of Blackmoor, Astley (1916-1963) became the Lancashire youths 1-mile track champion in 1936-37, the Harriers 3-mile youths track champion in 1935-37, and the Lancashire youths 880yds runner-up in 1936.
He was third in the East Lancashire youths cross country championship in 1936 and 37, and ran second in the St Helens & District cross county championship in the same years.

Arthur Farrimond, a veteran of distance running.
He was over 40 years of age when the above
photograph was taken during Leigh Harriers Sports.
In August 1935.

An unknown Leigh Harrier sprinter,
1930s.

Members of the Leigh Harriers cross country team during the late 1920s and early 1930s.

Jimmy Andrews, who joined the Harriers in 1922. He also had a talent for verse and writing dance music, some of which was published.

Jimmy Unsworth

Norman Thomas

Arthur Darwell

Leigh Harriers' sports meeting June 1928, the Mayoress accompanied by the Mayor, Mr Wm.Hindley, presented the award for the first event of the afternoon, the Northern Counties A.A. 10-mile track championships with fourteen entrants. The first mile was covered in 4min 49sec by Ernie Harper of Hallamshire Harriers, who was the eventual winner in a time of 54min 01sec. Second was W.Harrison of Earlestown Viaduct A.C., and third was Edward Rawlinson of Leigh. Harold Wood of Makerfield Harriers retired at the 3-mile mark owing to toe trouble.

Leigh Conservative Gala on the Athletic Ground 29th July 1933.
Lady Maureen Stanley crowning the Gala Queen, Miss Elsie Worthington of Atherton, behind the Queen are
Miss Eva Strong, Fabric Queen of Leigh and Miss Lois Heath, former Cotton Queen of Britain.

At Leigh open sports during the early 1930s, four of the sprinters are starting from the scratch mark in the 100yds handicap race. The two Salford A.C. athletes who ran first and second in the race are Walter Rangeley, pictured on the outside lane, with William Roberts in lane two.

One of Leigh Harriers last open sports meetings of 1935 was held on 17th August, the chief event was the senior men's 440yds Lancashire county championship race. The winner was William Roberts of Salford A.C. in 49.1sec, ahead of Tommy S.Dixon by 15yds he was followed by E.Fox of Manchester A.C. The above photo shows the Tyldesley senior boys school relay team, who won the 500yds race. The Mayoress of Leigh Mrs R.Starkie is seen congratulating the team on their success; the Mayor Robert Starkie is on the extreme left.

The boy's team left to right: K.Johnston, W.Oliver, J.Charlton, J.Colborne.

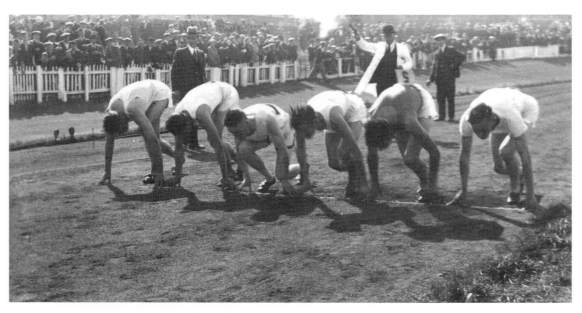

Albert E.Hayman starting the Lancashire 440yds Championship final at Leigh, 19th August 1933.

Walter Rangeley of Salford A.C. won by 2yds from lane one, with a time of 50.25sec. William Roberts, who was the reigning champion also of Salford A.C., ran second in lane four, and third was Sid Farrimond, from Bolton United Harriers in lane two.

The starter was Albert Edward Hayman, who was born 8th November 1886 in Leigh. He was a track cyclist in his younger days and in September 1909, he became one of the founder members of the present athletic club. In 1909 he began starting races at the Leigh track and by the 1920s and 30s was being noticed for his activities as an official starter in the Northern counties track championships and other similar events. One of the most prestigious sporting occasions in which he acted as an official starter, was at the British Empire games in London, August 1934. He was still one of the official starters at the club in the early 1950s.

During the First World War Albert was a Sergeant in the Home Guard. He re-married in 1927 after his first wife Ellen died, and had twelve children from his two marriages.

Albert was in the building trade all his life and was the first building manager for the Leigh Corporation. Two years before he died he resigned from the athletic club as Chairman because of his failing health; he died in Leigh, February 1954, aged 67, and was laid to rest in Leigh Cemetery.

Representatives from Leigh Harriers and N.C.A.A. Officials attended his funeral.

Walter Rangeley (1903-1982) of the Salford Athletic Club, pictured before running in the Lancashire 440yds final at Leigh, August 1933. Walter competed for Great Britain at three Olympic Games in sprint track events: 1924, 1928 and 1936.

British Empire Games commemorative bronze medal awarded to A.E.Hayman, for being an official starter at the games in London 1934.

Welsh Team & Positions

No 64	H.Gallivan	17th	
No.65	W.G.Mathews	15th	
No 66	A.Williams	18th	
No.67	D.Phillips	34th	
No.68	K.W.B.Harris	47th	
No.69	W.L.Raddon	45th	
No.70	G.W.Fox	33rd	
No.71	T.Richards	40th	Capt
No.72	C.Evans	46th	

Reserves

No.73	D.E.Morgan
No.74	E.Cooper
No.75	I.Brown

In the background is M.Gorman No.41 of Northern Ireland A.A.A. who was 19th

Belgium Team & Positions

No.13	Edouard Schroeven	26th
No.14	Pierre Bajart	37th
No.15	Louis Willemyns	44th
No.16	Rene Vincent	27th
No.17	Pierre Parent	32nd
No.18	Maurice Vandenberghe	35th
No.19	Oscar Van Rumst	7th
No.20	Rene Van Broecke	39th
No.21	Victor Honorez	—

Reserves

No.22	Gustav Maes	
No.23	Bert Hermens.	51st
No.24	Felix Meskens	
No.25	Roger Verbeek	

Scottish Team & Positions

No.52	Robert R.Sutherland	13th	Capt
No.53	J.C.Flockart	20th	
No.54	Wm.C.Wylie	22nd	
No.55	A.Dow	3rd	
No.56	John Suttie Smith	24th	
No.57	J.Campbell	30th	
No.58	W.J.Gunn	48th	
No.59	C.Smith	38th	
No.60	W.Sutherland	52nd	

Reserves

No.61	J.R.Farrell
No.62	P.McNab
No.63	W.Kennedy

113

Harold Eckersley with his trainer William C.Hughes, and the bronze "Maison Laffitte Trophy" which he was awarded for winning the international race at Ayr, Scotland, in March1928.

Harold's 1928 International Cross Country Gold Medal.

Bronze plaque awarded to each individual member of the victorious English International cross country team, Leamington Spa, 1930.

Harold Eckersley was born on 29th June 1903, at Earlestown, which is situated between the towns of Warrington and Leigh. He lived in the village of Lowton for the rest of his life only a couple of miles from where he was born. Harold had a choice of three local athletic clubs, Earlestown, Warrington or Leigh. He chose to compete for Leigh up to August 1920, then for Warrington A.C. until 1924, when he finally joined the Earlestown Viaduct Athletic Club.

In 1925 he was selected for his first international cross country race at Baldoyle racecourse in Dublin, and in 1928 he was selected again for the English team in a six country international at Ayr, Scotland, where he won the race.

Harold was in the coal business (Wilcock & Eckersley) when he married Ada Bent of Lowton in Sept 1931. He had many friends in and around the area; he lived on Newton Road until his death in August 1972.

England's cross country team at the Ayr racecourse, Scotland, 24th March 1928. No.16 is Harold Eckersley and standing behind him is Ernie Harper, the 1936 Olympic marathon silver medallist, who ran 7th for England. No.19 is William Beavers, who came in 6th position.
No.15 is Albert Worrall who ran 23rd, No.13 is Jack E.Webster. Others in the picture are H.W.Payne 5th, A.T.Muggridge 13th, and, holding the flag, is the president of the national cross country union in 1928, Mr J.Taylor.

List of Harold's Cross Country Achievements

1922	1st	West Lancs. juniors, Warrington
1922	1st	Northern juniors, Bramley
1922	2nd	National seniors, Hereford
1925		His first senior England Vest, Dublin
1926	9th	Northern, Newcastle upon Tyne
1928	1st	West Lancs Championships, Widnes
1928	2nd	Northern, Middlethorpe, York
1928	1st	England International, Scotland
1930	8th	England International, Leamington Spa

During his career he collected:
14 First prizes
10 Second prizes
 9 Third prizes

Earlestown Viaduct senior cross country team, pictured with the 1928 West Lancashire cross country team trophy. Harold Eckersley is on the back row, and on his right is William Atherton also a cross country international runner who competed at Brussels, Belgium, 28th March 1926.

Two-mile track race at Belle Vue, Manchester, 1930.

The Leigh lads are lined-up to the right of Harold Platt the Salford Harrier, who is pictured right of centre in the line up. The Leigh runners are R.Sutton, E.Rawlinson and J.Andrews. The starter is A.E.Hayman of Leigh Harriers, wearing the all white England strip in the centre of the line up is Harold Eckersley of Earlestown Viaduct A.C.

Leigh Carnivals and Galas held on the Athletic Ground, 1930s.

The Leigh Infirmary Carnival and May Queen took place on 13th May 1933. Thousands of people lined the streets and gathered on the athletic ground to see the winners in all the competitive classes. The above photo shows the fancy dress winners and humorous characters in the children's section, Zulu Chief, Lady Hamilton and Tutankhamen. Warm sunny weather prevailed through the afternoon but, unfortunately, heavy rain commenced about 5.30pm and put a complete dampener on the crowning of the May Queen, which had to be held in the Co-operative Hall.

The Leigh division Conservative Association held their gala show on 18th August 1934, on the athletic ground. The above photograph shows the newly-elected Gala Queen, Miss Mary Mullinger of Crawford Avenue, Tyldesley, being crowned by the Hon. Mrs Hornyold-Strickland, M.B.E. of Westmorland. On the left is the Rochdale Queen of Industry, Miss Nora Jackson, who was one of the judges.

Workers of the Astley Green Pit, who were also members of Leigh Harriers Athletic Club, won the Manchester Business Houses Cross Country Shield in March 1935.
Back row left to right: F.Sanderson, J.Y.Lloyd, J.Andrews, N.Thomas, J.Noon, J.Aspinall.
Front row : J.Unsworth, R.Sutton, E.J.Simms, H.Taylor.

The four counters for Astley Green Pit championship winning team, 1935.
Left to right: Richard Sutton 4th Norman Thomas 12th Jimmy Unsworth 11th Eddie J.Simms 6th.

Official programmes of the Manchester Business Houses Cross Country Association,
1933, 1934, 1935, 1936.

Jim and Joe training, ¾ Nelson on the athletic ground 1932

Joe Reid's main wrestling achievements
Bantamweight (124lbs = 56kg)

Empire Games	Canada	Silver	Aug 1930
Olympic Games	Los Angeles	Fourth	Aug 1932
European Games	Budapest	Fourth	Oct 1931
European Games	Paris	Bronze	Nov 1933
Empire Games	London	Bronze	Aug 1934

Lancashire Champion	1930-31-32-33-34-35
Northern Champion	1931-32-33-34
English & British Champion	1930-31-32-33-34-35

International match England Vs France at Hendon, London, Joe won his bout, May 1931.

In another match, this time between England and Belgium, at Brussels in 1933, Joe was the only English team winner in the match.

Joe did not travel to the 1932 Los Angeles games with the wrestling team, who were in the first party of the British Olympic squad to sail to the United States on the S.S.Empress of Britain,13th July. The reason being the team's Doctor was initially uncertain about Joe's fitness because he had a septic knee, however, he was given the all clear in time to sail with the second party which comprised of just the swimmers and boxers. They began their 6,000 mile journey from Southampton on the 20th July on the R.M.S.Majestic, a White Star Line ship. The party arrived in New York after a five day voyage, and then embarked on a five day train journey across the U.S. continent, completing their journey on the Santa Fe Railway and arrived in Los Angeles just in time for the opening ceremony of the games, on the 30th July.

Joe fought with the septic knee injury against A.Jaskari of Finland for the Bronze medal position, but lost the match to the Finnish champion in 7min 14sec.

Joe and the British team left Los Angeles on the 15th August, they sailed home on the S.S.Empress of Britain, and reached England on Friday 26th August.

127

Joe Reid at one of his many wrestling tournaments at Leigh, 1934

Joe and James Reid wrestling one another in the Lancashire Bantamweight wrestling championships at Leigh, 19th August 1933.

Joe Reid married Ethel Morley in February 1928, they had three children Marcus, Alfred and Teresa. From leaving school up to the outbreak of war, he worked at Chanters Pit, Atherton. During WW2 he served as a 'desert rat' Ammunition Driver in Egypt and Lybia, North Africa. His wagon was blown up by Rommel's Army at Tobruk in 1942, he was wounded by shrapnel, which lodged in his jaw, by 1943 he was stationed in Italy. Both of Joe's two sons also had sporting careers, Marcus became a well known professional wrestling champion, and Fred a top class track cyclist at Leigh from 1946 to 1957.

Saturday 19th August 1933, Joe Reid won the Lancashire county bantamweight wrestling championship belt for the fourth time in succession. He was then allowed to keep the gold and silver belt outright; it was worth £80.00 in 1933. Joe is seen above receiving the congratulations of the Mayoress on the athletic ground.
Also in the picture left to right are: James Langley Prescott (Mayor), Mayoress, John Dickinson the Athletic Club Secretary, Joe Reid, H.Hough runner-up from the Bolton Club, James Reid who came third for bronze, and far right Fred Brown the Harriers secretary.

The Lancashire wrestling championship was held in conjunction with the Leigh Harriers Open Sports. A good crowd turned up to the athletic ground to watch the days sport; with over 5,000 spectators in attendance.

Along with athletics, wrestling has also been a sport in which Leigh Harriers has gained the highest honours, with names like Harry Pennington the British, International and County Champion and Joe Reid who won a record number of British championship wins and who represented Great Britain and England in the 1932 Olympics, Empire and European Games.

Others were: Walter Mooney, William Jeffries, the three brothers: Tom, Jack and Bob Owen, Jim Grundy an English International and James Reid who had the rare distinction of wrestling his brother Joe three times in the English championship final. In other words during that period, Leigh Harriers had the cream of English amateur wrestlers.

Pictured on the left with Joe Reid is H.Hough of the Bolton Wrestling Club with his Lancashire bantamweight silver medal, August 1933.

Joe Reid, captain, with the other members of the Lancashire wrestling team, August 1933, on the athletic ground.

Joe Reid with his trophies in 1930, the year that he won the Lancashire and British Bantamweight titles and also represented England at the British Empire Games in Canada.

The British Empire Games silver medal that Joe won in Hamilton, Canada 1930.

Bronze commemorative medal that Joe received at the 1932 Los Angeles Olympic Games.

Joe Reid in 1930 with his winning trophies. Also in the picture are his two trainers, his father Jimmy, and on the left his father-in-law Abraham Morley.

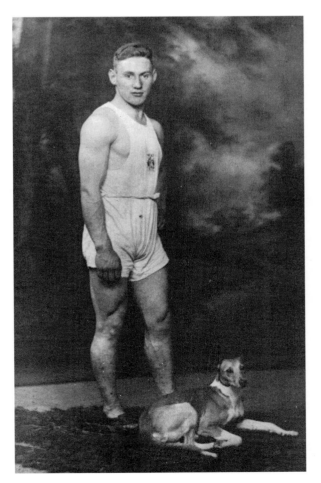

Jim Grundy had a mixed career in sport. He started his career with Bedford Hornets Rugby Club in the Leigh and District League when he was fourteen years of age. Two years later he was playing three quarter position for St Helens Recs, and he subsequently showed a talent for a place amongst the forwards; he weighed 12st 10lbs and stood 5'9".

Jim was speedy and trained with the Harriers' sprinters on the athletic track during the 1920s. In November 1926, he made his debut for Leigh R.F.C. at Keighley. He played eight games for Leigh that season and seven games the following season. He only scored one try whilst at the Leigh Club, during a game in March 1927 against the Wigan R.F.C.

By 1930 he had changed his sporting talents to a more solo event and had begun wrestling with the Leigh Harriers wrestling squad. By the summer of 1932, he had really started to take his new sport seriously, and in July that year, he became the runner-up in the Lancashire Heavyweight Championships at Atherton, where he was beaten by G.Gregory.

In January 1933 he was chosen to represent England at Light Heavyweight and by June, having trimmed down to middleweight, weighing 180lbs = 82.5 kg, he represented Lancashire against Yorkshire at Bolton and also fought in the National Championships at London the same year.

Jim is pictured on the left in his running gear in 1926. by 1935 he had become an all in wrestler.

131

The Leigh Harriers, three Lancashire Wrestling Champions 1931
Bill Jeffries - Lightweight   Joe Reid - Bantamweight   Tom Owen – Featherweight
William Jeffries 10st 5lbs =66kg
Lancashire County Lightweight champion .... August 1925, 1927, 1931.
Lancashire County Lightweight runner –up   1928, 1929
Lancashire County Featherweight champion-61Kg ....August 1928
English Lightweight Championship runner-up   1927 & 1931

William Jefferies was born in Glebe Street, Leigh, 13th August 1903. He worked as a miner and married Rachel Mayor 2nd September 1931 at the local Parish Church. They had one son, Roy, born in 1943. William died 15th May 1959, aged 55, and is buried in Leigh cemetery.

In June 1931, James Reid came fourth in the Lancashire Flyweight championship at Tyldesley. He had the rare distinction of wrestling his brother Joe three times in the English bantamweight final only to be beaten each time, the first time 1932, and then again in March 1933 in London.
James enlisted at the outbreak of war and was captured and became a P.O.W. in Malaya, where he lived on a diet of only rice. He wrestled the Japanese guards for cigarettes whilst he was captive, and because of the rough handling at the hands of the guards he became disfigured with cauliflower ears. James died in December 1989, aged 76, his wife Lillian died three weeks later leaving an only son Peter. As a youth James was part of the Leigh Harriers athletic team, seen above as a sixteen year old with his trophies wearing his athletic gear.

Sports programmes 1920-1951.

Olympic Athletes Compete at Leigh

**Ethel Johnson at the Leigh Harriers &
Athletic club open sports, August 1931.**

Nellie Halstead of Bury Athletic Club represented
Great Britain at the Empire Games, Canada in
August 1930, and was a member of the first British
women's athletic team to be sent to an Olympic
Games, competing in the 4x100m relay, in Los
Angeles, 1932. Other team members were Ethel
Johnson, Violet B.Webb, Alice G.Porter and May
E.Hiscock. Ethel and May were entered in the
individual 100m event, but with Ethel injured it left
only May to make the final where she ran fifth. In
the final of the 4x100m relay Nellie ran the anchor
leg bringing the team home for a Bronze medal and
in doing so they broke the previous world record.
At the British W.A.A.A. championships at Stamford
Bridge, July 1931, Nellie won the 100 and 220yds,
also broke the world record for the 440yds, and
again in 1932 with a time of a time of 56.8 sec.
She also held the 220yds world record in 1932, and
broke the British 880yds record in 1935.

In her later sporting years she played for the
Bolton Ladies Football Team and later turned to
Golf as a member of Lowes Park Club where she
was champion on several occasions.
During the Second World War Nellie worked as a
welder, and later worked for many years on a
cheese stall at the local market. Nellie died a
spinster aged 81, in Bury General Hospital following
a stroke, 11th November 1991. She is buried in the
family grave at Radcliffe Cemetery.

Miss Ethel Johnson was born at 116 Church Street,
Westhoughton, Lancashire, to Lawrence and Fanny
Johnson, on 8th October 1908. She was educated at
Hindley & Abram Grammar School, and later trained as
a teacher at Edgehill College, Ormskirk, Lancashire.
She taught at various schools and after the War she
became the Headmistress of the County School in the
village of Stalmine in the Fylde, Lancashire.
In 1927 her running career took off when she won the
Northern counties 100yds championship, followed by five
more Northern sprint titles whilst running for Bolton
United Harriers. At the W.A.A.A. championships in
London, July 1932, she set a world record of 11.0sec for
the 100yds, which stood as the record for sixteen years.
Ethel represented her country at the 1932 Los Angeles
Olympic Games in the 100m sprint but unfortunately she
sustained a leg injury in one of the early rounds,
preventing her from accomplishing her ambition of
breaking the Olympic 100m record. She competed at the
1934 Empire Games in London then retired from
athletics the following year.

After retiring from track athletics Miss Johnson was
actively connected with women's athletics in general, and
the administrative side of the Bolton United Harriers Club
in particular. In 1947 she was elected to life membership
of the club in recognition of services to the sport. Sadly
she died while visiting her home town of Westhoughton
in March 1964, and was buried in the town's local
cemetery.

**Nellie Halstead on Leigh Athletic Ground
August, 1933**

Ethel Johnson and Nellie Halstead running at the Bolton Utd Harriers A.C. sports, which was held at
Flapper Fold, Atherton, July 1932.

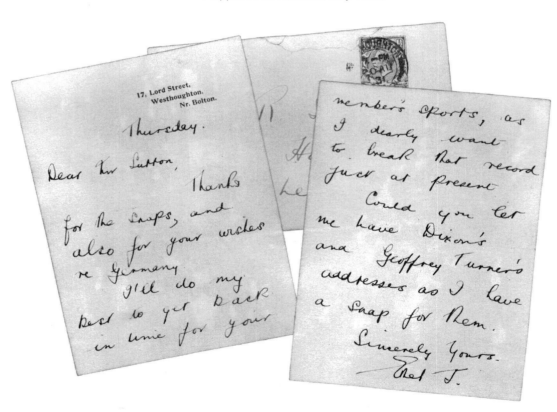

Letter postally dated August 1931, from Ethel Johnson to Richard Sutton the Leigh captain, thanking him
for the gift of photographs.

Mayoress of Leigh Mrs N.Fairhurst presenting the prizes for the ladies' 660yds relay, 17th May, 1930. Miss E.Johnson captain of the Bolton Utd Harriers team receives the award on behalf of the winning team with a time of 1min 22.3sec. The sports included the Lancashire senior men's 440yds championship won by Tommy S.Dixon, only 2,000 spectators watched the days sports.

Leigh Harriers sprinters at an unknown sports meeting. J.Banks, pictured centre, is the only known athlete of the three.

The Athletic Club retained the Leigh & District Social club Billiards League shield in April 1936.
In the picture Ald.W.Higginbottom, J.P., C.C., president of the league, is congratulating the captain of the team Mr Peter Cox on the team's success, along with other members of the team and officials of the club, John Dickinson, Fred Brown, William Miles Simpson, Chris Brown, Tom Collier and Harry Unsworth.

The 1-mile youths' Lancashire county championships held on the Leigh Harriers ground, 13th August 1936.
The winner was Tommy Cartwright of the Leigh club, pictured on the extreme left with 300yds to the finish.

Tommy S. Dixon, 1930.

Thomas Smith Dixon was born at 46 Ladies Lane, Hindley, on 28th November 1907, to William and Elizabeth. He was christened with the middle name of Smith, which was his mother's maiden name.

By the late 1920's he had matured into a promising athlete. As a member of Leigh Harriers at the age of twenty one he won the 1929 Lancashire 880yds senior men's final. He also won the Northern and Lancashire 440yds titles the following year.

On 16th May 1931 Tommy, who still lived in Hindley, succeeded in retaining the Lancashire 440yds championship on the Leigh Ground, in a time of 53.0sec. It was a thrilling race with E.H.Pilling of Manchester A.C. leading until the last few yards when, with a mighty effort, Dixon breasted home to gain a popular victory by inches. Third place went to W.Roberts of Salford A.C., who finished three yards behind.
The Harriers secretary gave a satisfactory sum for charity to the treasurer of the local Infirmary as a result of a good attendance of 5,000 spectators at the afternoon's sports.
Tommy married Hilda Kathleen Burrows in 1933, he gave up athletics and moved to Blackpool where they started a family before the Second World War. He retired from his occupation as a school teacher and remained in Blackpool, where he died aged 78 in June 1985.

Achievements in major races

1929	1st Lancs	880yds	2min 2.5sec
1930	1st Lancs	440yds	52.14sec
1930	1st N. Counties	440yds	52.15sec
1931	1st Lancs	880yds	2min 4.5sec
1931	1st N. Counties	440yds	52.25sec
1931	1st Lancs	440yds	53.0sec
1932	2nd N. Counties	440yds	52.0 sec

By June 1933, Tommy had joined Salford Harriers, and won the Lancashire 880yds championships at Bolton from F.R.Handley of Salford A.C. by only inches, in 2min 1.5sec.

1935	2nd Lancs	440yds
1935	3rd N. Counties	440yds
1936	3rd Lancs	440yds

Tommy at the 1932 open sports on Leigh Athletic ground.

Start of the Lancashire 440yds final, 17th May 1930, at the Leigh Harriers Ground. The winner by 5yds was Tommy S.Dixon of Leigh Harriers pictured centre, in 52.14sec from W.Rae of Broughton Harriers. In third place was H.Stourton of Old Mancunians. Because of the heavy rain at the start of the sports, only 2,000 spectators turned up to watch.

The above photo, taken at Leigh Harriers sports, Sat 17th May 1930, shows Tommy S.Dixon of Leigh Harriers being congratulated by the Mayoress on winning the senior men Lancashire county 440yds championship, which he also won the following year. The Mayor of Leigh, Mr Novello Fairhurst, is in the centre of the picture and Tom Collier the Harriers official is wearing the bowler hat.

Charles F.Madely, pictured above in 1938, joined Leigh Harriers in 1936 as a sixteen year old and was a notable sprinter in his youth.

Charlie became the Harriers Secretary in 1962 and remained so for over 20 years. During that time he became one of the figure-heads of the club; he carried out the administrative duties and the maintenance of the athletic ground and track. Charlie was well known in the Leigh area, he ran along the town streets practically every day for fifty years long before hot showers and the running boom of the 1970s.

Sadly, Charlie died in Feb 1988, he is still talked about with fond memories by the club's older members who knew him. After his death the Charles St athletic ground was named Madely Park in memory of him.

Charlie, pictured above in the summer of 1947, winning the Harrier's open sports 100yds, running on the inside lane against his fellow team mates, in a time of 10.89sec.

Charlie won many local track races before and after the Second World War. He is pictured above in 1947, at home with some of his prizes.

The Leigh Harriers 1938 sprinting team, pictured on the Charles Street ground.
Charlie is pictured standing centre and Teddy Roberts far right on the back row.

The Leigh Open Sports, 14th August 1948, guest runner and winner of the 100 and 220yds races was Edward Haggis the Olympic representative for Canada. Haggis ran the 100yds in 9.9sec, beating the Harrier's track record set by W.R.Applegarth in 1914. Haggis was staying with his aunt, a Mrs Carter of Leigh Road, Howe Bridge, Atherton, for the period of the Olympic Games. Charlie can be seen running on the inside lane for 2nd place in 10.6sec.

The Leigh Open Sports, 30th July, 1949, final of the Harriers 220yds open handicap, Charlie was given 2nd place behind R. Finch of Earlestown who won off the14yds mark with 22.1sec, 3rd F.Ethridge of Barrow A.C. Although it rained throughout the afternoon the sports were attended by over 3,000 spectators.

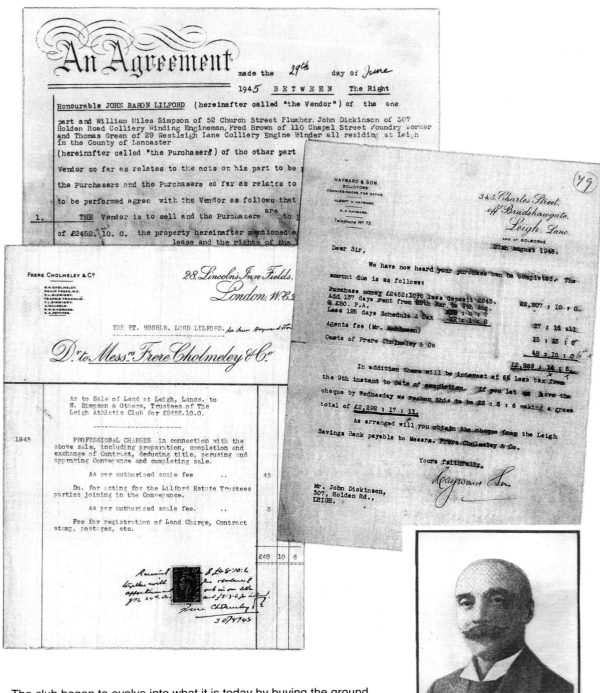

The club began to evolve into what it is today by buying the ground outright on the 29th June 1945. Benefitting from the increased membership, the club managed to raise the money to pay the final agreed purchase price of £2,452, for the 4¼ acres of land, to the Right Honourable John Baron Lilford.

The persons who made and signed the deal on behalf of the club were the trustees: W.M.Simpson, J.Dickinson, T.Green and F.Brown, all who lived in Leigh.

Mr Albert Harris Hayward (1868-1955) pictured above, was a Leigh solicitor and the Secretary of Leigh Infirmary 1905-1920. His firm Hayward & Sons, acted as official solicitors for the Harriers' purchase of the athletic ground from Lord Lilford in 1945, they had dealt with the early land leases during the 1920s and 30s. Albert Hayward was No.1 Platoon commander in the Leigh Athletes volunteer force from 1914-1919 (see photo on page-38) His two sons, George and Cecil, were members of the athletic club before the First World War and George, a commissioned officer, served with the Manchester Regiment as Lieutenant.

The Leigh Harriers and the Leigh R.F.C. agreement for the 1946-47 season.

After the war, the Leigh R.L.C. wanted a larger and better ground to play their matches on. The suggestion was to build the new ground, Hilton Park, on Kirkhall Lane. However, this was delayed as the land was being used by allotment holders, and their agreements did not expire until 1946. Therefore in the 1946-47 season, having nowhere to hold heir home matches, the club approached Leigh Harriers for temporary use of their ground, until the Hilton Park ground was completed, an agreement was drawn up and as a result the Harriers were unable to hold any track meetings that year.

Leigh rugby players in action, pictured in two different matches on the athietic ground during the 1946-47 season, the precise dates are unknown.

159

Letters from Lord Liford's Land Agent, Mr J.A.Robinson to the General Secretary of the Athletic Club Mr John Dickinson, during the 1920s, 30s and 40s.

In 1947 the Leigh R.L.F.C. new ground 'Hilton Park' was completed.
The Harriers ground in Charles Street reverted back to Athletics.

Start of an 880yds race at Leigh, 1948
Left to right: Unknown, Syd Isherwood, John B.Whitfield, unknown, Eddie J.Simms, Charlie F.Madely at
the rear and an unknown starter.

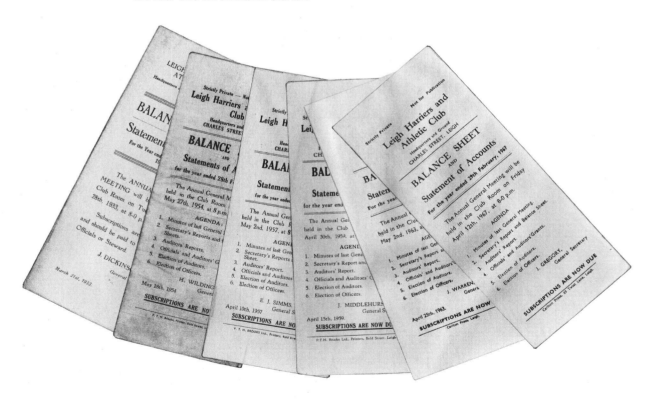

Harriers account sheets from 1933-67, showing the names of six General Secretaries.
J.Dickinson 1933, H.Wilding 1954, E.J.Simms 1957, J.Middlehurst 1959, J.Warren 1963, J.Gregory 1967,

Leigh athletes warming-up before a track sprinting session 1949-50.
Only three names are known, Alan R.Bond, Charlie F.Madely and Arthur Nixon.

The Harriers 4x100yds relay team at an unknown athletic sports meeting during the middle to late 1940s.
C.F.Madely, unknown, T.Prescott, B.Baldwin

Stan J.Fell from Atherton with his trophies, August 1946.

Stan was a member of the inter-counties winning cross country team for Lancashire 1952 and1954, and gained a team gold medal when Bolton United Harriers won the national in 1954.

Stan won the club's 1,000yds Harry Brown shield from 1946-51. As a youth he collected a bronze medal at the unofficial East Lancs cross country race at Ratcliffe, 24th February 1945, and he was the first youth home in an unplaced team. He won the Harriers' winter track 3-mile youth champs in 1946, the junior 7-mile champs in 1948-49, and the 10-mile senior championship for the John Horrocks cup in 1951. In 1952 he joined the Bolton United Harriers club, where his running achievements continued.

Leigh open sports 21st May 1949, Stan Fell is seen running in 7th position on the last lap of 880yds race. The winner was M.Bell of Bolton Utd Harriers in 1min 53.6sec, with Stan just behind him for second place.

John Bailey became the clubs 100yds junior and senior champion for the W.Shaw cup in 1949, he was also the 1949 Lancashire County junior sprint champion over 100yds.

Alex Gaskell won the schoolboy 100yds Macnamara cup in 12.48sec at the club championship sports 1946.

Leigh Harriers group at a Bolton track meeting, July 1948

C. W.Salmond	A.M.Jackes	E.Haggis
1,500m	High Jump	Sprinter

The above Canadian Olympic athletes competed at the Leigh Harriers open sports, on Saturday 14th August 1948, when they should have been attending the Olympic closing ceremony in London.

Edward Haggis of London, Ontario, was brought over from Canada by the Warrington R.L.F.C. in Dec 1949 and was given a three month trial period on the Warrington A-team. He played a good game against the Wigan A-team in February 1950 at Central Park, and at Wilderspool against St Helens in March. He scored the first try of the match, helping the Warrington A-team to a 21-6 win.

In April he returned home on the Empress of Canada saying he would not be returning, but expressing his gratitude to the local people who had made his stay so pleasant. His only regret was that he would not be with the club the following season, he had fond memories of a fine club and the greatest bunch of supporters that any team could possibly have.

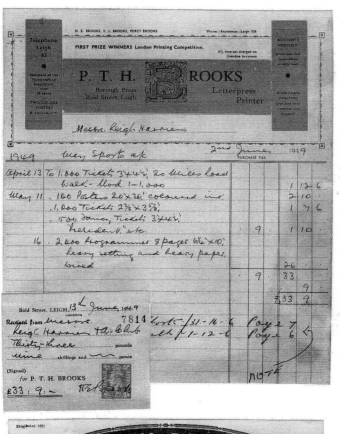
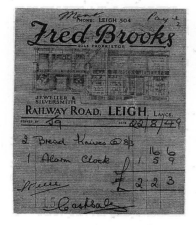

Leigh Harriers' receipts from: Perrins gift shop, Collins & Darwell printers, Brooks the jewellers, Leigh Friendly Co-Operative Society Ltd, Guest Bakeries on Manchester Road and P.T.H. Brooks for posters, tickets and 2,000 sports programmes.

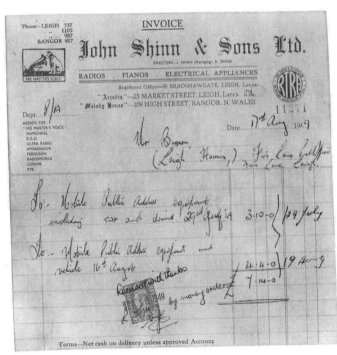

John Shinn & Sons Ltd provided the Leigh Harriers with the electrical equipment required for the sports days i.e. microphones and speakers etc. for the sports announcements. The top photograph was taken in the 1950s, after the shop had relocated from Market Street to Queen Street.
Bob Royle was always in attendance at the Sports Days, providing the spectators with ice cream refreshments.

Roy Hilton with his trophies in 1949.

Roy lived with his parents at the Leigh Conservative club in 1948, until he went to Aberystwyth University.
In 1947 and 48, he was the Leigh Harrier's junior and senior 100yds sprint champion and the junior bronze medallist for the 100yds at the1948 Lancashire track and field championships.

Whilst a student he had some notable successes:

1948	3rd	Lancashire 100yds Junior
1948	1st	100 & 220yds University College of Wales
1948	2nd	220yds Welsh University Championships
1948	3rd	100yds Welsh University Championships
1949	1st	100yds Welsh University Championships
1949	3rd	220yds Welsh University Championships
1949	3rd	100yds Welsh University South Wales Vs London
1951	2nd	100yds & 220yds University of Wales
1951	2nd	100yds & 220yds Welsh University Championships
1951		Selected for Welsh University Vs Wales Vs English Universities

Leigh Harriers presentation night, held in the club house, 13th February 1949.

The three main trophies awarded that evening were for the best up and coming stars:
Connie Bolton best female athlete, Reginald Grundy best male athlete, and H.C.Glen best cyclist from the Manchester Clarion Club.
Note, also in the photograph are Fred Norris and Alan S.Danson, who both became Olympians at the 1956 Melbourne Games.

Winter Track Championship awards January 1948

A.E.Hayman, one of the founder members of the present athletic club, presented the trophies to the winners: E.J.Simms 10-mile, S.J.Fell 7-mile, J.Ramsden 3-mile.

The officials in the picture are Matt Thorpe standing at the back, and the four trustees of the club, Fred Brown, Thomas Green, John Dickinson and William Miles Simpson standing on the far right.

Albert E.Hayman starting the track league one-mile handicap race at Leigh, early 1950s.

Harriers sports programmes and membership cards, 1924-53.

Past Presidents of the Leigh Harriers Athletic Club

Reproduced courtesy of Wigan Heritage Service

George Shaw Esg J.P.
Mayor of Leigh 1900-01
President of Leigh Harriers
1909-11

William Harrison Esq J.P.
Mayor of Leigh 1908-09
President of Leigh Harriers
1912-19

Sir George Holden, Bart J.P
Mayor of Leigh 1920-22
President of Leigh Harriers
1920-27

John Horrocks J.P
Mayor of Leigh 1924-25
President of Leigh Harriers 1928-46

Herbert Gough J.P.
Mayor of Leigh 1939-41
President of Leigh Harriers 1947-54

Fred Norris British Olympic Athlete

Start of the Harriers 10-mile track championship, 29th Jan 1949
C.F.Madely, E.J.Simms (2nd), J.B.Whitfield, F.Norris (1st), A.J.Taylor (3rd)

Fred Norris became the national cross country champion in 1959, the northern champion in 1953,54 & 59, and the East Lancashire champion in 1954, 55, 56 & 60.

The final 220yds of the club's 10-mile track championship shows Fred Norris beating the veteran athlete E.J.Simms by 11sec, in a time of 57min 33sec. Fred's trainer Syd Isherwood, is seen here on the inside of the track, keeping an eye on his progress.

Signed photograph of Fred and his son Edmund, training whilst they were living in Boston, Massachusetts in 1964.

Fred Norris handing over the baton to Stan Fell, during the Manchester to Blackpool road relay, May 1954.

Fred Norris was born on the 4th September 1921, at Primrose Street, Tyldesley, Lancashire. After leaving school in 1935 he worked in a machine shop, and later at Cleworth Hall colliery as oil and greaser, until 1960. He married Doris Birch in July 1944, they had one son Edmund, who became a champion athlete himself whilst living in America. Fred's interest in sport was playing football for his local team but after watching a newsreel of the 1948 London Olympics at the local cinema, he decided to take up running and joined Leigh Harriers. The following year, under the guidance of Syd Isherwood, he won the Harriers 10-mile track championship and won it again in 1950. He joined Bolton United Harriers in 1951.

The records set by Fred from 1953-62 totalled 68, he held English, native, Empire, all-comers, national and world best times during his career; on occasions he broke his own record achievements.

Fred broke track, area and course meeting records at various distances from two miles up to the marathon, he represented his country at the British Empire Games, European Championships, cross country internationals and the 1952 and 1956 Olympics. How such a fantastic performer, one of the best Britain has ever produced, got such meagre publicity in the national press remains a mystery.

In the 1958 A.A.A. championships the 10-mile track race was revived after an eleven year gap, Fred won the race in 49min 39sec, beating Billy Eaton's (of Salford Harriers) record set in 1936 by nearly one minute, the following year he again broke the championship record with a time of 48min 32.4sec.

He won the East-Lancs cross country championship at Royton in 1960, where he was presented with a special gold medal by Mr Harry Whatmough the East Lancashire President, for winning the 1959 Northern, National and International cross country championships races.

Fred and his family emigrated to Louisiana in September 1960, where he gained a University Scholarship, the family later settled down in Boston, Massachusetts. Whilst in the U.S. Fred received the accolade of being the elected president of the Lancashire C.A.A. Mr C.Rice said of the nomination :-
"Fred's never failing loyalty to the association has been a constant source of inspiration to all Lancashire athletes, teams and officials, who are proud to salute him as their President".

Fred won 43 of his 44 races during his three year running career in America, in 1962 he held the world's best time for the 1-mile for the over 40s age group at 4min 21sec, and also won the Canadian Marathon championship in the same year.

Not only did Fred win the Washington Hill road race, summit 6,288ft in 1962, but he set a new record and, being over 40 years of age, he also set a veteran's record, his time being 1hr 4min 57sec. In the year 2000, $4,000 was offered to anyone who could better Fred's time, but no one did. In 2001 the stakes were raised to $5,000 and in addition four pacemakers were provided. This time Fred's record was broken by a few seconds, but it had taken 39 years for this to happen.

Fred and his wife moved back to Tyldesley from Boston in September 1986, Fred always said that he would never have been able to train as he did had it not been for his wife Doris, who had always supported and backed him up throughout his athletic career. Sadly, Doris died two hours before her 80th birthday, January 2003.

There is a typically nice story of Fred's sportsmanship, which happened in the 1961 Boston Marathon when he was running against former champions Eino Oksanen and John J.Kelly. Just before the hills a stray dog charged onto the course and sent Kelly sprawling onto the pavement. Norris stopped to assist Kelly and, in doing so, lost valuable time and forfeited his chance to win the race. Kelly finished runner up to Oksanen. Unexpectedly, Fred died in Dec 2006 following a fall in his home town of Tyldesley, he was 85 years of age.

Syd Isherwood pictured with Fred Norris and Geoff Saunders, of Bolton Utd Harriers Saunders was the winner of this cross country international, 1951.

Fred's 1952 Olympic participation medal.

Fred seen here in his Lancashire vest, on the Leigh Athletic ground in 1950. Lancs won the Inter-counties cross country championships in 1949-52.

Thirty six year old Fred Norris receives a framed colour print of himself from his colliery workmates, May 1959. He was one of Britain's finest long distance runners and was the first Britain to cover more than 12-miles in one hour, achieved on 28th April 1956, at Walton-on-Thames, a record only Heino and Zatopek could then equal.
On the left is the 1914 National cross country championship trophy (Chesham Challenge Cup).

Bolton members of the Lancashire cross country team, January 1951
Jack Haslam, Geoff Saunders, Walter Berry, Jeff Eastham, Fred Norris.

The English 9-mile cross country championships at Warwick, March 1956. Seen here leading at the
3-mile stage is Fred Norris who finished 2nd, being followed by No.386 Ken Norris the eventual winner in
48min 11sec, beating Fred by 6sec. Tracking them closely behind is Derek Ibbotson, the following July
Ibbotson broke the Australian John Landy's world record for the 1-mile with 3min 57.2sec.

Fred in his coal mining days.

Winning the 1959 English counties 20-mile road championship at London, breaking the course record by nearly 7min.

Running along Manchester Road, Tyldesley, January 1959.

Fred Norris, Walter Hesketh, D.R.Gordon Pirie, at one of their many cross country meeting during the 1950s.

Winning the 1959 National cross country championships at Peterborough.

Fred leading the 1958 English inter-counties cross country championships from Ken Norris, P.B.Driver and G.D.Ibbotson. Fred was sent the wrong way when leading by 50yds and eventually finished in third position.

Sir Fred Longworth after hearing that Fred Norris had been chosen for the 1952 Olympic Games. Ald. Longworth, who was a Lay Preacher had christened Fred in 1921. Fred is holding the shield he won at the A.A.A. Championships.

H.Jack Sixsmith won the Harriers 4-mile cross country cycle race from Golborne to Leigh in November 1950.

Seen here participating in the Harriers 25-mile time trial, on his Claud Butler racing bike, along the Leigh section of the A580 (East Lancashire Road) in the early 1950s.

H J.Sixsmith won the Harriers half-mile cycle track championship in 1950, with a time of 1min 10.8sec. Seen left at the start of a pursuit race on the Harriers track, 1948.

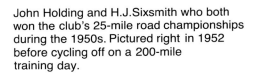

John Holding and H.J.Sixsmith who both won the club's 25-mile road championships during the 1950s. Pictured right in 1952 before cycling off on a 200-mile training day.

Ken Coan the Harriers cycle track champion seen on the left competing in the Harriers 25-mile time trial, along the Leigh - Lowton section of the A580 in the early 1950s.

Ken Coan being presented with the 1953 Harrier's 880yds cycle championship 'Fallowfield Cup', from the club's President Ald.Herbert Gough.

Leigh track sports programmes 1948-1955.

Leigh Harriers track league prize presentation for the runners and cyclists, October 1952.
Front row left to right: Iris Millington, Joyce Baines, Joan Prescott, Evelyn Disley, 2 unknowns, Margaret Lightfoot, Alan Spencer Danson, unknown, Fred James Howker
Back row: Unknown, Alan R.Bond, Jimmy Billington, John H.Nicholson, Teddy Roberts.

Start of a track cycle race at Leigh 1952. Ken Coan on the outside lane was the winner.

Ken Coan pictured in 1956 with many of his cycling trophies.
Ken was the Harriers 880yds track cycle champion from 1952-1956.

Leigh Harriers open track meeting 1952.
Left to right: Alfred Reid, Terry O'Neill, Ken Coan.

Leigh Harriers open 5-mile event, 1953. The picture on the right shows the cyclists on the bend just after the start, with Ken Coan overtaking the group on the outside.

Cyclists line up for a track race at Leigh, 1952-3 season.
In the white shirt is Ken Coan of Leigh Harriers, with the support of Ronnie Ayres.

On Ken's left is R.D.Brewer of Altrincham, who rode for the Manchester Wheelers Club.

Preparing to start the 500yds race at Leigh, 1952-53 season. Ken Coan the Harriers track champion is on the inside lane.

196

Harriers 880yds championship scratch race, 26th July 1950.
On the inside lane is the Harriers 1950's club cycle champion Ken Coan, who finished the championship race in runner-up position. Jack Bretherton in lane two with the support of Fred Reid. In lane three D.Griffiths with the support of N.Bonner, in lane four Terry O'Neill , in the outside lane is the winner Jack Sixsmith supported by Charlie Halliwell.

Leigh Harriers championship sports, Wed 26th July 1950
Devil take the Hindmost (invitation race), winner was L.Jackson of Manchester Wheelers, in 7min 6.2sec.
In 2nd place was R.A.Geldard of Manchester Wheelers and 3rd B.Barnes of Westwood R.C.

Leigh cyclists dressed as young tramps, before their Sunday morning outing from Leigh Market Square, November 1951. The two senior cyclists are James Leonard far left, and Ronnie Haseldine far right.

Leigh Harriers cycle team 1952
Left to right: Jack Woods, Joe Wildman, Ronnie Ayres, Jack Baxter, Terry O'Neill and H.Jack Sixsmith.

Leigh Harriers Trophy Winners , October 1950.

On the left is Teddy Watkins (walker), from the Earlestown and Lancashire walking clubs, who won the best male athlete of the year award.

Noreen Gregory of the Leigh club (track athlete and high-jumper), won the best female athlete of the year award. Right is Alan Spenser Danson, who won the cycle track league silver trophy for the Wigan Wheelers Club. Alan was born at Wallgate, Wigan, on January 25th 1928. After the war he worked as a fitter at the Triangle Valve works at Lamberhead Green, and lived at Redwood Avenue, Orrell, Wigan. During the late 1940s and early 1950s he and his Wigan Wheeler team mates trained hard on the local roads and he collected many prizes from around the county.

By 1952 Alan had joined the Manchester Wheelers Cycling Club and had competed thirteen times internationally for England against France, Bulgaria, Germany and Ireland, gaining twenty seven firsts and numerous second placings for England. In December 1956 he rode for Britain at the Melbourne Olympics in the 1,000m time trial event, where he finished in fifth position, breaking his own British record for the event with a time of 1min 12.3sec. The only Wigan cyclist to achieve Olympic medal status was Benny Jones, who represented Britain at the 1908 London Olympics and won two golds and one silver medal.

Alan held several British records during his cycling career: the 1,000m standing start, the half-mile standing start, the one-mile event, the quarter-mile standing roller record and the half-mile flying start.

In Jan 1957, he married Betty Glover of Orrell, at St Johns Church, Pemberton, in August 1958 they emigrated to Australia where Alan worked in a hobby shop, but also made a living through sculpting. His wood carvings sold throughout Australia, America and Canada. Alan was praised by the Australian people for his art work and some of his beautiful wood sculptures still stand in the Canning City Council Chambers, Perth.

As a result of a brain tumour, Alan died in his sleep in Perth, Western Australia, on the 16th August 1988, aged 60. His widow Betty brought Alan's ashes back home to England and scattered them in the grounds of St.Lukes Church at Orrell. Betty died in January 1995 in Wigan; they had no children.

Alan's Olympic blazer, tie and hat are in the National Cycling Museum at Llandrindod Wells, Powys, Mid-Wales, they were donated by Alan's sister-in-law and the Wigan Wheelers club. However, two of Alan's cycling medals, programmes and cycling photographs are in the Leigh Harriers collection, donated by Alan's sister-in-law in 2008.

Leigh Harriers Festival of Britain open sports, 26th May 1951

An easy win by Alan, in the 500yds sprint final. He almost threw the race away by easing up and was nearly overtaken on the line by D.Gee of M.A.C., and R.Bardsley of Manchester Clarion.

The 1,000yds sprint cycle final, Alan makes no mistakes this time!

Alan's wedding day, 26th January 1957,
St Johns Church, Pemberton, Wigan.
Alan is wearing his Olympic blazer and
tie.

Alan training at the Olympic Velodrome, Melbourne,
November 1956.

Three-mile point-to-point race at Nelson, Lancashire,
26th September 1953. Alan finished 4^{th,} starting off the
scratch mark.

One of Alan's wood sculptures made
of jarrah a Western Australian
hardwood. All of his art work was
sold in Perth after his death in 1988.

Leigh Harriers Athletic Club Members at the annual awards evening, held inside the club house, October 1950.

1	Alan R.Bond	15	Harry Ellicott	29	Gordon R.Goodwin
2	Alf J.Taylor	16	Mr Fell	30	J.Wynne
3	Arthur Nixon	17	Unknown	31	Albert E.Ayres
4	Jack Kinsella	18	Fred J.Howker	32	Matt Thorpe
5	Johnny Sixsmith	19	Jack Whittaker	33	Teddy Watkins
6	Larry Newton	20	Evelyn Disley	34	Connie A.Bolton
7	Ronnie Howarth	21	Laurie King	35	Noreen Gregory
8	John Bailey	22	Olwyn Hodkinson	36	Alan S.Danson
9	Derek R.Howarth	23	Unknown cyclist	37	Joan Prescott
10	Margaret Turner	24	Unknown cyclist	38	B.Aldred
11	Unknown cyclist	25	Ken Coan	39	Edna A.Buxton
12	Mable Leach	26	Unknown cyclist	40	Unknown
13	June Haigh	27	Unknown cyclist	41	Unknown
14	Sid Lightfoot	28	B.Wynne	42	Unknown

Track league prizes and awards, set up in the Harriers stage room, October 1950

The track league awards, Stage Room October 1950
Left to right: Tommy Prescott, Teddy Watkins, Stan J.Fell, Connie A.Bolton, Noreen Gregory, Olwyn Hodkinson, Ken Coan, Alan S.Danson, H.J.Sixsmith.

Old programmes from 1909-1950, which still survive and can been seen in the Leigh Harriers museum archives. The 1948 programme is signed by the two Olympic cyclists Alan Bannister and Alan Danson.

Harriers trophy winners and officials, October 1952
Back row left to right: Don S.Holt (sprinter), Frank Evans, Roy Greenwood of Heywood Wheelers,
Mr Joseph S.Clare president of the National Cyclist Union Manchester Area, Brian Whitfield (walker) and
Fred J.Howker who was the race starter and Track League President.
Front row left to right: Matt Thorpe, Evelyn Disley and H.Winstanley (equal point winners),
Teddy Roberts and Albert E.Ayres (cyclist).

Frank Evans, the British Olympic 800m runner, just back from Helsinki, presented the prizes to the
Harriers track league winners inside the club house, October 1952.

The Festival of Britain Celebrations May and August 1951

The August event was organised by the Leigh Parks Superintendent Mr I.L.Davies, and a selected committee who arranged special seating arrangements to accommodate the spectators. During the intervals and between races, musical items were played by Leigh Borough Band and entertainment was provided by the acrobatic clowns of Sheffield, The Barratt Bros.

The jockeys who took part in the Donkey Derby were: W.Nevett the Northern champion, J.Thompson, D.L.Jones, W.Snaith, J.Dyson, V.Mitchell, J.Egan, H.Greenway, R.Sheather, J.Caldwell, D.Buckle and M.Pearson, all of whom had been engaged at Haydock Park race course that same afternoon. The mounts were sand donkeys brought from Wallasey, New Brighton and Southport.

The stewards were the Mayor of Leigh (Counc. William Woolstencroft J.P.), Counc. Mr J.Breese, Mr E.Collier and Mr J.R.Travers. At the Liberal Hall Ball later that evening, prizes were presented to the winning Donkey Derby jockeys by Mr Ben Howard Baker from Liverpool, the former Everton, Chelsea and England goalkeeper. Baker was British high-jump champion and record holder in his younger days and had represented his country at the 1912 and 1920 Olympic Games.

Dagenham Girl Pipers, who gave displays on the Leigh Athletic Ground as part of the Festival of Britain celebrations, May 1951.

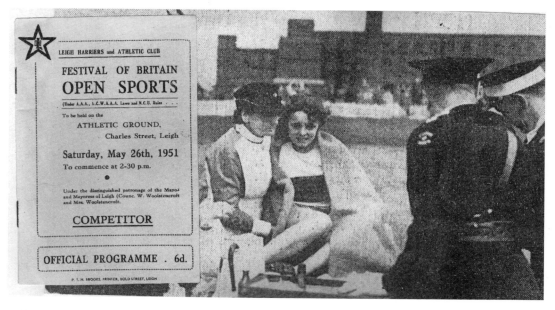

At the Festival of Britain open sports, Leigh, May 1951, Connie A.Bolton of Leigh Harriers receives treatment from the St John Ambulance Brigade after suffering an ankle injury.

Start of the Donkey Derby, Bradshawgate Chase, at Leigh Harriers Wed, 15th August 1951, part of the Leigh Festival of Britain celebrations, with 8,000 spectators present.
Two saddles were empty within 20 yards but the race continued accompanied by the sound of shaking rattles held by the jockeys, and the shouting of the crowd. The race was won by J.Caldwell riding Quality Street, and owned by Mr T.Flynn a local grocer.

On the final bend of the second race, the Plank Lane Selling Plate, the field was well strung out but the leaders ran off the track to allow the second group of riders to come through and win. There was so much excitement in this race that the stewards forgot to get the second donkey home.

Derek R.Howarth winning heat-3 of the 100yds open flat handicap, 26th May 1951.

Final of the100yds senior mens open flat handicap: 1st J.E.Butler Earlestown Viaduct A.C. off the 10yds mark, in 9.7sec, 2nd W.Ashley Sutton Harriers off 6½yds, 3rd Derek R.Howarth Leigh Harriers A.C off 9yds, and 4th B.Gibson of Salford Harriers A.C. off 6yds.

Derek Howarth wins the 440yds at Leigh 26th May 1951

Walter Hesketh pictured on the right of Manchester A.C. winning a 3-mile invitation race at Leigh in 14min 46.5sec, 19th May 1951. He returned to Leigh the following week and won the 1-mile race handicap by 2yds, starting off the 110yds mark in 4min 06sec.

Below, the Lancashire senior 7-mile cross country championships held on 7th January 1950. The Harriers president Ald. Herbert Gough J.P. started the race at the Hall Farm Estate, in the village of Culcheth.
The picture shows the eventual winner, No.8 Geoff B.Saunders of Bolton Utd Harriers, next to him is Walter Hesketh of Manchester A.C., who was still a junior and ran second, there were 110 starters in the race.

Walter Hesketh (1930-2007) was the National & Northern senior cross country champion in 1952. He was one of only two athletes ever to win national cross country titles for youths, junior and senior men.

209

Leigh Harriers Athletic Team 1952
Back row left to right: K.Isherwood, J.Kinsella, L.King, C.F.Madely, S.Isherwood, A.J.Taylor and the
brothers V & T.Nestor.
Front row left to right: J.Settle, J.Isherwood, T.Prescott, D.R.Howarth, A.R.Bond, D.S.Holt, K.Tabenor.

Start of the first race of the cross country season, the runners are lined up on the corner of Charles Street
and Holden Road, Leigh, October 1951
.**Left to right :** V.Nestor, E.J.Simms, C.F.Madely, unknown, S.J.Fell, B.Horrocks, D.Pyke who was the
handicap winner, A.J.Taylor, J.Hutchinson, A.R.Bond, C.Heaton, G.Blacoe, unknown.

Lancashire Walking Club Officials, 1950's
Left to right: Harold Mills, Billy J.Jackson - Chairman & Judge, Mrs Smith - Timekeeper,
Harold Willcox - Timekeeper & Judge, Joe Lambert - Treasurer & Judge.

Inter-club match at Leyland, 30th August 1958.
The above photo was taken along Back Lane, Leyland, which was re-named Langdale Road after part of its route was changed to accommodate the building of the M6 motorway.
Left to right: Ron Wallwork, Mike Jeffreys and Jack Sankey all of the L.W.C. and R.Howarth of Leyland motors.

Winner of the Hindley Green 7-mile walking race, J.L.Barraclough of the Lancashire walking club, who led from start to finish, is seen above congratulating Jack Sankey of Leigh Harriers, who came in second place. Brian Whitfield of Leigh is pictured standing between them, November 1957.

Northern area 10-mile walking championship at West Didsbury, 1st February 1958.
Left to right: Jack Sankey 3rd of the Lancashire Walking Club, F.Winter 1st of Sheffield Utd Harriers and Terry J.Hardie 2nd also of the Lancashire Walking Club.

Leigh Harriers open sports, Saturday 26th May 1951, Jack Sankey leading in the early stages of the 1-mile walking race.

A close finish at the end.

The North Lancashire junior 1-mile champion Brian Whitfield, being disqualified by the official Mr Bill J.Jackson, on his last stride to the finish line.

227

Start of the junior and senior men's Northern area 10-mile walk, at the Red Cat Inn, Hindley Green, Leigh, 1959.

Finishers approaching the finishing line, passing the Red Cat Inn.

Ted Watkins 5th
Lancashire Walking Club.

Abe Holland, 2nd
Sheffield Utd H. Walking Club.

D. Slynn, 3rd
Sheffield Utd H. Walking Club.

The Harriers road walking championship, with members of the Lancashire Walking Club, starting outside the Harriers ground on Holden Road, Leigh, 1st November 1963.

The sixteen walkers, heading along Holden Road towards Platt Fold cross-roads, November 1963.

Lancashire Walking Club training session at Leverhulme Park, Bolton, 1962.
Left to right: Ivor Percival, Frank O'Neill, Mike Hatton, Sam Shoebottom, Eric Hall, Tony Taylor, Martyn Trotman, Ron Wallwork, Jack Sankey, Joe Lambert, Julian Hopkins, Ted Watkins and Dick Smith.

Jack Sankey, finishing fourth in the Northern area 20-mile walk, on a wet and windy day in Morecambe, 27th April 1963, the year of his retirement from serious competitive walking.

The following three photographs where taken at the drinks station at the St Anne's stage of the 1962 Manchester to Blackpool road walk race, approx 8-miles from the finish.
The race was promoted by the Lancashire Walking Club.

Alf and Tony Taylor are pictured handing out drinks Bob Miller of the U.S.A. and Frank O'Neill.

No.17 Chris Bolton refusing a drink from Bob Loude.

Officials, Alf and Tony Taylor, handing out drinks to Burras of the Yorks Walking Club and to Jack Todd.

The last 50m of the Leigh Harriers open sports 5-mile walk, August 1970, which was filmed by the BBC. Ron Wallwork of the Lancashire Walking Club and Bolton Utd Harriers, was the fastest over the 5-mile course in a time of 36min 09sec.

Pictured above wearing his 1963 International vest, Ron Wallwork aged 29, at the Leigh sports, August 1970. He had just returned from the Commonwealth games held in Edinburgh, where he competed for England and finished 5th in the 20-mile walk, 18th July 1970. He was selected to represent his country at the 1966 Commonwealth Games in Jamaica in the 20-mile walk, where he won Gold for England.
In 1971 Ron broke the U.K. 2-hour record; covering over 16-miles he was the first Briton to break the 16-mile barrier.

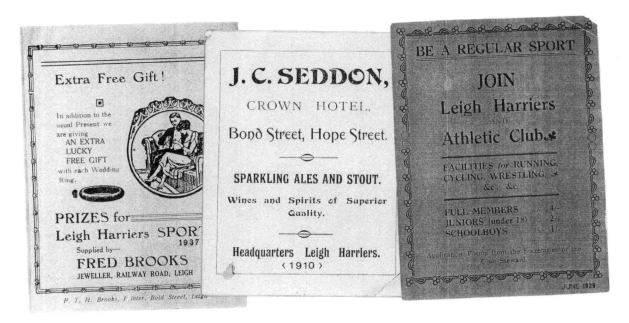

Sponsors of the Harriers track sports, Jim C.Seddon of the Crown Hotel, Bond Street, 1910.
Fred Brooks Jewellers on Railway Road, 1937. Also a sports advertisement which indicates that people could join the Harriers athletic club by subscriptions of 1/- to 4/- June 1929.

Four cross-country championship programmes which are in the Harriers archive collection:
Lancashire 1957, Northern 1959, East Lancashire 1948 and the Northern 1951.

The Leigh Harriers track championship awards were presented by Mr Eustace Collier J.P., 23rd July 1955. John Anthony Byrne is being presented with the 880yds junior cup; he also ran second in the English Schools 1-mile and was the1955 Lancashire schools 1-mile champion.

Leigh Harriers Track Champions July 1955
Left to right: Vivienne Hughes 80yds schoolgirl champion, Jack Sankey 1-mile walk champion,
Ken Coan 880yds cycle champion, Alan Riddings 100yds schoolboy champion, Jimmy Billington 100yds
junior champion, Edna A.Buxton 100yds ladies champion, John Anthony Byrne 880yds junior champion,
Don S.Holt 100yds senior champion, Alan R.Bond 1,000yds Harry Brown Shield,
Allan Grundy 2-mile boys champion.

Miss Edna A.Buxton receiving her prize from Mr Eustace Collier J.P., for winning the ladies 100yds handicap, Edna also received her gold medal for the ladies 100yds club championship, July 1955.

G.Charnley announcing the winner of the 100yds schoolboy championship, Alan Riddings, who broke the club record with a time of 11.4sec, seen receiving his gold medal from Mr Eustace Collier J.P.
Mr Collier also donated the Eustace Collier cup in July 1955 for the 440yds schoolboy relay, which he presented to Allan Grundy the Leigh Grammar School Captain.

Don S.Holt receives his trophy from Mr Eustace Collier J.P., for winning the senior mens 100yds sprint championship, in a time of 10.4sec, whilst Teddy Roberts selects the medals, 23rd July 1955,

100yds handicap race at the Leigh Harriers track league,1954. On the outside lane is D.R.Howarth, off the scratch mark is Don S.Holt, the sprinter on the inside lane is unknown.

Leigh Harriers cross county team, who won the boys Aaron Trophy, Leeds, November 1956.
Robert Ferguson, Beverley Bolton, Allan Grundy.
It was the first time that a Lancashire club had won the event and the Leigh lads won by 30 points, from 32 teams. Two days later they were informed that Sheffield had won and Mr Ted Roberts, the Leigh Secretary, was asked to return the cup. However, he demanded to see the results sheet and two days later he received a postcard saying "keep the cup, we have found an error", he also received an apology from the officials explaining it was "the first mistake in ten years."

Beverley Bolton won the boys cross country race at Leeds. Beverley is the younger brother of David Bolton who played stand-off for the Wigan rugby league team in the 1950s. In July 1956 Bev became the first under-15s boy in England to break the two minute barrier for the 880yds, which is 4.68m further than the 800m run today, his time was 1min 59.9sec which he achieved at the English Schools Athletic Championships at Plymouth, he finished second; the boy who beat him was over 15-years of age.

Ladies

Up to the 1970s the club never had a very strong ladies section, although in the 1930s they did have Ada Parker and Lew Davies, the two sprint champions, also the high-jumpers Eileen Smith and Ethel Quinlan who was the runner-up at the 1932 Northern championships.

The late 1940s & 50s brought young sprinters such as: Connie A.Bolton, Hilda Winstanley, Margaret Lightfoot, Edna A.Buxton, Mabel Leach, Olwyn Hodkinson, Jean Marsh, Joan Prescott, Joyce Baines and Evelyn Disley. Also Molly Lightfoot, who achieved success as a walker and became the Northern Counties 1-mile track walk champion in 1950.

In the 1960s the club had Pat Mooney the county sprint champion, Valerie Guest and Lesley Evans, county and British schools champions, there was also Susan Taylor, Pauline Whittle, Sandra Heaton, Joan Baldwin, Jean Barlow, Pat Green and others who always gave a good account of themselves, especially in relay races.

On the left is Valerie Guest, and right is Pat Mooney both pictured in 1963. In June 1963 Valerie became the Northern Counties 100yds champion and runner up in the 150yds junior championships at Stanley Park, Blackpool. She also became the Lancashire 100yds and 150yds sprint champion for Leigh Harriers during that year.

Leigh Harriers ladies 4x110yds relay team 1953
Left to right: Edna A.Buxton, Hilda Winstanley, Joan Prescott and Margaret Lightfoot.

Lew Davies (centre) was the Leigh Harriers 100yds sprint champion 1932-33, pictured above with her new team mates Dorothy Manley and Ethel Johnson (sitting right) in 1934, the year Lew moved to Bolton Utd H.

Leigh Girls Grammar School were the inter-schoolgirls track & field champions, pictured above on the Manchester Road playing fields, June 1962.

Left to right: Joan Fallon, Leslie Howarth, Lesley Evans, Valerie Guest, Pat Thornton and Marlene Clare. Lesley Richards, nee Evans, won the English junior schools 70yds hurdles in 10.2sec, July 1963. She was also the Lancashire schools sprint hurdles champion in 1963, 1964 and 1965, and became a junior international against Canada. Lesley had to give up her sport because her job clashed with her training nights, she became a journalist for the Leigh Reporter 1966-70, she then became Sub-Editor of the Wigan Evening Post and the Wigan Observer, then Editor of the St Helens Star 1973-76, and the Leigh Reporter 1977-96. She retired in 1996, but returned as a columnist for the Leigh Journal in 1998.

At the charity sports promoted by Leigh Harriers in May 1931, Ada Parker, pictured on the left, ran second in the ladies 100yds sprint race, behind the British international runner Nellie Halstead of Bury Athletic Club.

Ada was the Leigh sprint champion in the early 1930s; she was also the club's record holder at the 100yds with a time of 11.8sec. Lew Davies later broke her record before joining Bolton Utd Harriers In 1934.

Leigh Harriers Annual Championship Trophies, 1958.

1.   Senior men 1-mile track walking - G.R.Goodwin Trophy
2.   Senior men 880yds track cycling - Fallowfield Wheeler Cup
3.   For the best male athlete of the year.
4.   100yds ladies sprint cup
5.   100yds junior Men sprint cup
6.   Senior men 10-mile track - John Horrocks Cup.
7.   Junior men 880yds track running - F.King Cup
8.   Harriers 1,000yds running - Harry Brown Shield
9.   Unknown
10. 2-mile schoolboys under 15s cup
11. 100yds schoolboys - G.Cooper Macnamara Sprint Cup
12. 100yds senior men sprint - W.Shaw Cup
13. For the best female athlete of the year, early 1950s
      later used for the junior men 7-mile track championship.
14. Youths 3-mile track running cup.
15   2-mile boys running championship cup.

Start of the ladies open 80yds handicap race on the athletic ground early 1950s.

Eric J.Haslam winning the club's 880yds handicap race for boys under 16 from E.Grundy, in 2min 13.7sec. 21st June 1958, Eric also won the 2-mile race.

The final of the club's 100yds junior sprint championship, 21st June 1958, the winner was John Booker in 10.8sec. He also won the senior men's race with the same time; in 2nd place was C.Heaton and in 3rd A.Hay.

First lap of the junior 600yds handicap race, 21st June 1958.

The final few yards of the junior 600yds handicap, the winner was Alan Bailey followed by Allan Grundy and John Booker.

The Harriers trophies ready for presentation to the track runners and cyclists, 21st June 1958.

Beverley S.Bolton of Duke Street, Wigan, is being presented with the 880yds junior club championship trophy by the Mayor of Leigh Mr Fred Taylor, 21st June 1958.
Bev was the Wigan Grammar School cross country junior champion in April 1955. He was also the runner-up at the northern schools cross country championship from 422 starters at Lyme Park, Disley, Cheshire, 16th March 1957, he covered the 2½-mile course in 12mins 11sec, and finished only three seconds behind the winner, Butler of Middlesborough.
At the East Lancashire cross country championships, Royton, the Leigh boys team finished 2nd in the 2-mile race from 14 teams with 94 starters, 9th February 1957.
Beverley Bolton ran 3rd followed in by Robert Ferguson 4th, W.Leadbetter in 15th and Alan Bailey 19th.

Harriers Jubilee Celebrations on the Charles Street ground, September 1959.
Standing left to right: Harold Wood, J.Cartwright, Charlie F.Madely, Maurice O'Neill,
Stan Culpin, Pat Mooney, Syd Isherwood, Roy Wood, Eric J.Haslam, unknown, Eric Grundy,
Derek R.Howarth, Jack Charlson, Bob Baldwin.
Kneeling: Alf J.Taylor, Len Whittle, Robert Ferguson, John Johnson, Ted Roberts,
John Keith Gibbins, Chris Hallinan, Edward John Rawlinson, Bill Horrocks, Brian E.Jackson.
Sitting: Unknown, Noon, Billy Wilkinson, D.Ward.

The Mayor gets ready to fire the gun to start the youngsters race at the Harriers Jubilee celebrations,
September 1959.
Left to right: John Dickinson, Jack Clarke, Ted Roberts, Mr James Sumner (Mayor),
John Johnson, Eric J.Haslam, Stan Culpin, Roy Wood, unknown, D.Ward, Noon,
Billy Wilkinson, Mick Fhay, Tony Taylor, and John K.Gibbins on the inside lane.

Eric Haslam in 1965; winning the 1-mile event for Loughborough college, against the A.A.A. select team in 4mins 10secs.

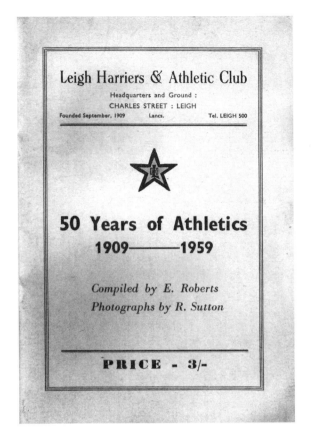

In September 1959, the club produced a 40 page booklet listing the club championship winners from 1909 to 1959, the booklet includes five photographs.

In 1964 the club continued to produce a steady flow of junior champions, however, the emphasis had switched from track athletics to the social club with its bar and bingo nights.
It was therefore surprising that the Athletic Club shrugged off take-over enquires for the athletic ground, from the nearby Electricity Board, various building companies and the local council.
The president of the club Mr Jack Clarke, who had been a member since 1920, the Harriers' secretary Charlie F.Madely, and the other members of the Harriers committee decided to make more of an effort in rebuilding an athletic spirit within the club.

The committee began by having the boundary fence replaced , which had fallen into disrepair so a new £700 concrete boundary wall, a brick built changing room equipped with showers, and also gave the athletes the benefit of a fully qualified, A.A.A coach for a short period of time.
The old Atherton Brook, which flowed along the southern perimeter of the ground, was filled in by the Mersey River Board, giving the club the opportunity to re-enlarge the running track back to over 400 yards. The corner stone of the committee's rebuilding programme was to secure a grant to help with the track extension and build up gradually from there.

The officials of the cycling section did make a tentative enquiry about the prospects of re-introducing cycle racing at the athletic ground, but they were told that they would have to do most of the cycle track renovations themselves. The cycle track was in such a poor condition that it would have taken 12 months work to restore it to a satisfactory standard; the cyclists had insufficient members and funds to complete the necessary work. Although the Harriers cycling section continued to use the club house as their headquarters for many years after that, they could only hold road racing events.

Dick Sutton presenting the house relay shield to the senior champions, Agnes Rudd and Raymond Longson, at the 25th annual sports at Westleigh County Secondary School, Wed 31st May 1961.

There were ten records broken that day. Richard Sutton, who presented the shields and trophies, was a Leigh Harrier, and international cross country runner in 1929. For the past 24 years he had acted as starter for the school sports. It was to be his last time at presenting the awards as, in the following years Charlie Madely of Leigh Harriers had the honour.

Leigh R.L. Captain Bev Risman, with his wife, presented the medals and prizes at the club championships, 13th June 1962.

Harriers runners warming up for the club's Harry Brown Shield 1,000yds championship, June 1963.

Only three athletes ran in the 1963 1,000yds championship.
Inside lane: Chris Hallinan (Senior) who ran second, Eric J.Haslam (Junior) won the race in a new club record time of 2min 20sec; 3rd was John McFarlane.

Eric J.Haslam 26th June 1963, receiving his award from Mr F.J.Howker for breaking the club's 1,000yds track record in 2min 20sec. A month later he also won and broke the English Schools 1-mile junior track record in 4min 11.4sec.

Presentation of the club championship prizes in June 1963. Eddie Pavitt, the 100yds sprint champion, receiving his prize from the race starter and N.C.A.A. official, Fred J.Howker the Harrier's chairman.

Chris Hallinan running 2nd in the club's 1,000yds championship, 26th June 1963.

Fred J.Howker, acting as starter for the Harriers 80yds school-girls sprint final, 4th June 1960. The winner was Margaret Fildes.

Frank Briscoe wins the 880yds Leigh Grammar School sports, 3rd June 1964, in a record time of 2min 1.8sec; he also won the 1-mile race. Frank is the nephew of Thomas Briscoe the Harrier's 1929 junior 1-mile champion.

Leigh Harriers winter track championships awards, January 1963.

N.C.C.A. timekeeper Jeff W.Settle presented the awards to the 2, 3, 7 and 10-mile champions.
Boys 2-mile: M.Johnson, S.Riley and W.Makin who was only 12 years old.
Youths 3-mile: F.Briscoe, C.Fairclough, W.Cartwright, L.Poyser, W.Stokes.
Junior men 7-mile: E.J.Haslam, E.J.Rawlinson.
Senior men 10-mile: R.Ferguson, C.Hallinan, B.Horrocks.
Others in the photograph are: K.Hindley, J.Burns, J.Cartwright, B.Baldwin, E.Roberts.

The Leigh Harriers winter track championship awards, January 1964.
Track champions left to right: R.Ferguson, F.Briscoe and K.France.
Others on the photograph are: P.Fenwick, L.Poyser, E.Ranicar, B.Stokes, J.Burns, M,Johnson,
W.Cartwright, E.J.Rawlinson, M.O'Neill, B.Horrocks, E.Roberts, and C.Hallinan.

The club's 100yds senior championship final, June 1964.
1st Eddie Pavitt, 10.3sec, 2nd Brian Grundy, 3rd John Hooson, 4th Derek R.Howarth, 5th Tony Green.

The final of the 220yds championship, June 1964.
1st Eddie Pavitt, 2nd Brian Grundy, 3rd Derek R.Howarth, 4th John Hooson, 5th Tony Green.

Final of the 100yds Harriers junior championship sprint, Wednesday evening, 17th June 1964.
1st John Hooson 10.9sec, 2nd D.Leatherbarrow, 3rd Tony Green.
John Hooson was the Harriers youths and junior sprint champion from 1963-65. In 1963 and 1964 he was the Lancashire Schools 220yds champion. He ran second in the 1964 Lancashire Schools 100yds, and came 4th in the English Schools 220yds final at Hendon. In 1965 he won the Lancashire A.A.A. Junior 220yds championship at Warrington. John also played rugby for the Leigh Schoolboys, but unfortunately had to give up his sporting career following a motorcycle accident in October 1965, in which he suffered a serious leg injury.

Leigh Harriers track champions with their trophies June 1964.
Back row left to right: F.Briscoe, T.Taylor, T.Aspinall, J.Hooson, E.Pavitt, P.Whittle.
Front row: Leigh schoolboys 4x110yds relay champions, Leigh Grammar School, in a time of 52.2 sec, D.Jones, R.Fletcher, S.Dootson, S.Crisp.

St Mary's R.C.School won the boys' under 15's 4x110yds team relay, on the Leigh Harriers ground and became the Leigh school boys champions in June 1961. The above photograph was taken later at their school, Manchester Rd, Astley.
Left to right: Unknown, R.Ridgeyard, B.Wilkinson (captain), M.Savin, F.Stirrup (reserve).

Leigh Harriers group on the athletic ground, summer 1965.
Some of the faces known are: Derek, John, David and Gail Howarth, John A.Gerrard, Malcolm Johnson, Michael Madely, Eric Holcroft and Paddy Kelly.

Paul Baines aged 11, Paul Jameson and Michael Madely aged 10, and 13 year old Steve Howcroft, preparing to take part in Leigh Harriers 4th track league meeting of that year, August 1969.

The Liverpool to Blackpool road race, 25th July 1964, run over a distance of 48½ miles.
It was the third longest race in the world at that time. Pictured leading the race, just outside Preston, is Leigh Harrier Chris Hallinan, who finished 2nd in the race with a time of 5hours 33mins 30secs (he had run 3rd the previous year). The winner was No.2 Bernard Gomersall of Leeds, and 3rd was Barry Fletcher of Wakefield Harriers. Bill Horrocks was the 2nd Leigh Harrier home, finishing in 12th position; helping Leigh Harriers to win the second team prize.

The English Schools track and field championships were held at Hendon, Middlesex, 17 and 18th July 1964.
The Leigh representatives, seen in the above photograph, left to right, are: Mike McNeil senior-boys
100yds sprint, Frank Briscoe senior boy's 1-mile, Lesley Evans intermediate girl's 80yds hurdles,
Graham Gleave 1,000yds steeplechase and John Hooson intermediate boy's 220yds sprint.

Final of the Leigh Harriers Senior Men 100yds championship, Wednesday evening, 17th June 1964.
No.19 E.Pavitt, No.21 B.Grundy, No.1 J.Hooson, and D.R.Howarth.

Leigh Harriers Open Sports and Inter-club Meeting 21st August 1970
Filmed by the BBC documentary team.

First lap of the inter-club team race over 3,000m. The Leigh lads in the picture are Kenny Peers on the outside in 6th. Frank Briscoe the eventual winner is pictured in 9th place, and, just behind Frank, is Warren Greenhalgh who finished 4th.

The second lap of the 3,000m.

There were 12 athletic clubs represented in this race:
Mid-Cheshire, Winton, Pilkingtons, Bolton Utd Harriers, Wallasey, City of Stoke, Manchester & District, Warrington, Oldham, Farnworth, Stretford and Leigh Harriers.

Frank Briscoe in the last 20m of the inter-club 3,000m team race. He won in a reasonable time of 8min 49secs.

298

Start of the 1-mile open race.
21st August 1970

Second lap of the 1-mile race,
all finished as in photo order:

1st Frank Briscoe of Leigh H.A.C,
(County Champ) 4min 12.2sec.

2nd M.Bateman of Manchester &
District, 4min 17sec.

3rd Colin Roberts of Leigh H.A.C,

4th Roy Wood of Warrington A.C.
(formerly of Leigh H.A.C.)

John A.Gerrard, who had joined
the Sale Harriers Club from
Leigh Harriers only a few
months earlier, won the 800m
race in 1min 53.8sec.
Frank Briscoe, his previous club
team mate, finished just behind
him with a time of 1min
54.1sec.
M.Kirkman of Bolton Utd
Harriers came 3rd in time of
1min 57.4sec.

A false start by John Wilding of Leigh, on the inside lane in the 100m open race. 21st August 1970.

An even start on the second time of asking in the final of the 100m. The winner was Barrie Kelly, the Bury international in lane four, in a time of 11.0sec. 2nd was Eddie Pavitt of Leigh in lane five, in a time of 11.2 sec, and 3rd was P.Cornes of Warrington A.C. in 11.4 sec.

Barrie Harrison Kelly, 100m Olympian in 1968, was the winner of the 100m inter-club race at the Leigh Harriers Open Sports and Inter-Club meeting, 21st August 1970. He was an international sprinter of the Bury & Radcliffe Athletic Club and became the A.A.A.100yds champion in 1967 with 9.9sec. He was also the A.A.A. indoor champion at 60yds in 1966 with 6.3 sec, and the A.A.A. 60m champion in 1972 in a time of 6.8sec.

No. 59 Ian Eggleston, the Harriers Treasurer in the early 1970s, running at the Stretford open meeting, 1971.

Lancashire A.A.A. County Championship at Kirkby Stadium, Liverpool, May 1970.

Leigh Harriers 4x400m relay team: Jim Prescott, Colin Roberts, John Wilding, John A.Gerrard, Eddie Pavitt. The team just missed out on medals in 4th position. Colin competed in the 3,000m and acted as a reserve for the relay team.

Change-over from J.Prescott to E.Pavitt in the 4x400m relay, Kirkby Stadium,1970.

Annual Lancashire County Road Relay Championship Southport Sept 1970

Taken before the start of the 8 x 3½ -mile Southport road relay.
Left to right:
Kenny Peers, Joe Cooke, Maurice O'Neill, and Jim Prescott.

Kenny Peers tags to Colin Roberts on the 1st leg.

One of the later legs of the Southport road relay, 1970. Ian Eggleston of Leigh hands over to John Wilding.

Leigh Team at Southport 1970,
Left to right:
Joe Cooke,
Kenny Peers,
Joe Galvin,
Jeff Fielding,
Ian Eggleston,
Colin Roberts,
Chris Hallinan,
John Wilding.

The Leigh team finished in 18th position.

303

The Harriers Track Championship June 1970, with the St John Ambulance Brigade on standby, they had attended every sports meeting at the Leigh track since the early 1900s.
The timekeepers are: John A.Gerrard, Chris Hallinan and Jeff W.Settle.

The first change over at the National road relays championships, at Blackpool 6 x 4-miles, October 1970. The Leigh runners are Jim Prescott No.158, and Kenny Peers No.157.

Peter Glass handing over to Joe Galvin at the change-over mark. Bolton Harriers were the championship winners, the Leigh team finished in 21st place. The two Leigh team members not pictured are: Colin Roberts and Maurice O'Neill.

Leigh Harriers annual christmas party 1970, held in Mr Armstrong's Restaurant above the Electricity Board Shop on Bradshwagate, Leigh. The photo shows the following committee members with their wives: Derek R.Howarth, Fred Gaskell, Harry Hulme, Jeff Fielding.

A group of Leigh Harrier's members, August 1970, shown in the photo are Shelagh Devine, Fred Gaskell, Diane Lomas, Charlie F.Madely, John and Ian West, Warren Greenhalgh, Eddie Pavitt, and six unknowns.

A Selection of Photographs from Leigh Harriers Track Championships, June 1970.

Charlie Madely and Derek Howarth organising the young boys 80m race.

Just after the start of the 800m boys race.

The girls 80m sprint final.

The boys 80m sprint final, Paul Jameson and Michael Madely.

Fred Norris turned up at Tyldesley C.E. School on 15 August 1956, to show his official invitation to the Olympic Games in Melbourne. His son Edmund is standing behind his father with his hand on his shoulder. Mr R.Horsfield, the headmaster chose some of the schools young athletes for the group photograph.

Geoffrey Turner relaxing at the Amsterdam Olympic Games, 1928. Note - his official Olympic competitors badge on his blazer lapel. In 2009 the new Leigh Sports Village was officially opened by the Queen and Duke of Edinburgh, and one of the new roads, leading to the Leigh Harriers (New Madely Park) athletic stadium is named after him, 'Turner Way'.

Geoffrey Turner with the British Amsterdam Olympic Team posing for the official photograph at Southampton Dock, July 1928.

Geoffrey Turner photographed with the England's International Athletic Team at Stamford Bridge, London. France Vs England match, 30th July 1927.

Joe Reid pictured with the Great Britain Olympic team, standing on the dining hall steps at the Olympic Village, Los Angeles, 1932.

Pictured left, Thomas Briscoe the 1929 Leigh Harriers junior 1-mile champion. He also played for the Leigh R.L. club's first team, in the late 1930s. (1911-2003)

His nephew Frank Briscoe, was a cross country International, the 1974 Southern C.C. Champion and the 1975 Northern C.C. Champion.

Tommy W.Gorse standing on the left wearing Bolton Utd Harriers colours, 1930-31 cross country season, the year he resigned from the Leigh Harriers club.

Ellis Green, Harriers Sec, in the 1920s. Pictured above taking part in the Bedford Church play, 1937, as "Von Mark".

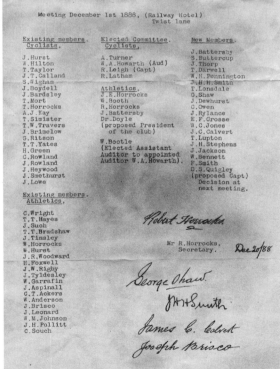

A.E.Hayman official starter, pictured centre, at the Salford Tramway track sports, 1914.

Sprinters James Quinn and John Hodgson captain of Tyldesley R.U.F. team, 1920-21

Leigh Harriers (unknown) female athlete, pictured on the athletic ground. 1930s.

Austin Littler winning the Lancs 1- mile junior championship at Irlam, Aug 1933.

Leigh Harriers Intermediate Ladies, 4x110yds relay team, E.A.Buxton, M.Leach, C.A.Bolton and J.Haigh, May 1950.

Stan J.Fell, Charlie F.Madely, Margaret Lightfoot and John Bailey at an early 1950s track meeting.

Connie A.Bolton, July 1949.

Donald Bond, July 1949.

Roy Hilton, sprinter, 1948.

Photograph above shows the start of the 1922 Surrey walking club's Croyden-Godstone-Croyden race. The 1924 Olympic silver medallist Gordon Reginald Goodwin who moved up to Leigh from London in 1910 is indicated by the X.

COMPETITOR.

71st ANNUAL FESTIVAL
......OF......
Wenlock Olympian Games,
WHIT-MONDAY, MAY 28th, 1928.

1850   1928

WILLIAM PENNY BROOKES
Founder Wenlock Olympia Games, 1850, and Pioneer Physical Education.

May this Society that he hath founded,
In the old town, in which he lived and died,
In the dim future ever be surrounded
By those who make it, for his sake, their pride.
Annie Moore, Wolverhampton.

PROGRAMME   -   PRICE 3d. EACH.

Sports programme for the 1928 Wenlock Olympian Games, which is in the Leigh Harriers archive collection.

William Penny Brookes (1809-1895) was the man behind the humble beginnings of the Olympic ideal, he was was a burly, bearded doctor who devoted himself to improve the lives of the people in his home town of Much Wenlock. It was his idea to revive the Olympian ideal that was to have a worldwide impact and lead to the modern Olympics. His vision for the Olympic Games is hailed as one of modern sports greatest achievements.

Baron Pierre de Coubertain was almost certainly inspired to create the global games festival after a fact-finding mission that led him to the small town of Much Wenlock in Shropshire. It was while Coubertain was watching the Much Wenlock Olympian Society's games held every year in the town, that he realised the potential for the modern Olympics. Although Brookes died months before the Athens 1896 Olympics, aged 86, much of what happened at the first Modern Olympiad was based on his ideas.

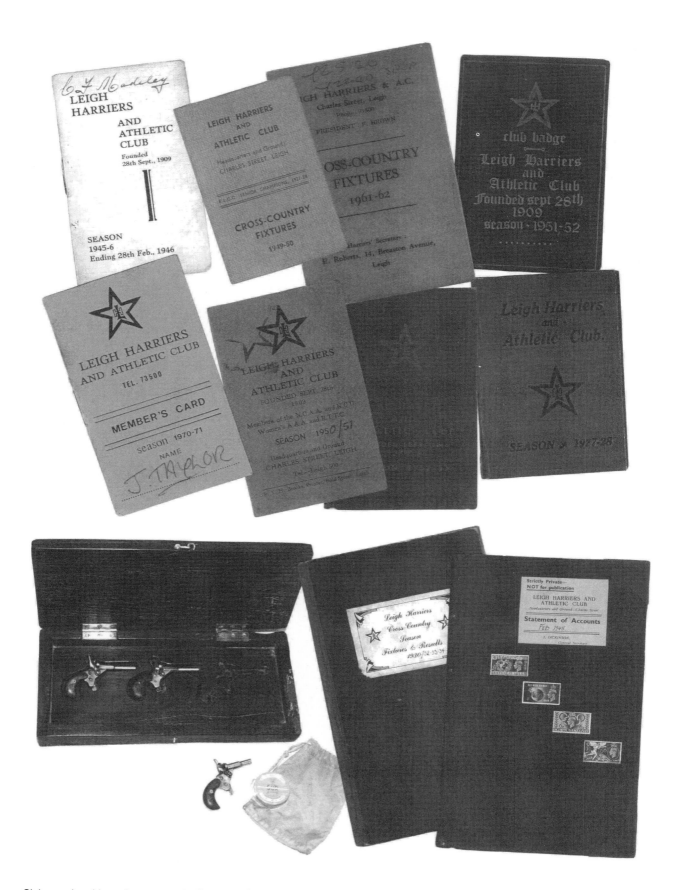

Club membership and cross country fixture cards, 1927-71. Starting pistols used for the athlete's starting practice during the 1920s and 30s, which belonged to Matt Thorpe of Leigh Harriers dating back to the 1890s. Two club ledger books, one dated early 1930's containing results and cross country fixtures, and one from 1948-50 containing the Harrier's club accounts.

Acknowledgements

This book would not have been possible without the kind permission of Mary Sutton, who has allowed me to use her late father Richard's collection of Harriers' photographs for the compilation of this book.

I owe a special thank you to Sarah Marsden (Pippa), for many hours spent assisting, connecting and refining the pages of text and photographic contents of this work. The book would not have been finished if it was not for her kind unselfish time and effort in assisting me to prepare this book for publication.

Thank you to Len Hudson for the contribution of his photographic expertise, and to the local History Officer at Leigh Library, Mr Tony Ashcroft for his knowledge and patience, in helping me with my constant enquiries.

I would also like to thank Alan Bailey, Neil Shuttleworth, and David Smith for their encouragement and guidance, and for their expertise on proof reading this work. Despite all the assistance I have received in completing this book, any mistakes, I must claim for myself. A final thank you to Mrs Ida Allison for her help in the final stages of this publication. Appreciation to Wigan & Leigh Leisure & Culture Trust for waiving the reproduction fees.

I am grateful to all the people listed below, who have been very helpful to me in piecing together the information and the historical background of the photographs, and to all those who have in anyway contributed to the completion of this publication.

Eddie Almond   (Race Walking)
Albert Aspen M.B.E. (Olympian Wrestler)
Derek Aspinall
Paul Baines
Margaret Bates (nee Clarke)
Tarasa Baxendale (nee Reid)
Ken Beevers (Local Historian)
Jack Betney (Northern Vets. President)
Bolton Olympic Wrestling Club
Phillis Boydell (nee Pennington)
Dr Frank Briscoe O.B.E. (A.A.A. International)
The late, Thomas Briscoe (Rugby & Athletics)
The late Ian Buchanan (Olympic Historian & Writer)
Brian T.Bullock
Vera Burke
Joe Cartwright
Terry Casey (Leigh Rugby)
Eileen Castledine
Ken Coan (Cycling)
Lindy Cocharan (nee Sutton)
Edith Coleman
Les Cooke
The late, John Corbett (Boxing & Wrestling)
Linda Curry
Karen Dewitt (nee Birchall)
The late Geoff Doggett, (Salford Harriers)
Joanne Farrimond (nee Battersby)
Stan J.Fell
Bill Friar (WW1 Historian)
Joe Galvin (Leigh Harriers Chairman)
The late, Fred Gaskell
Roy Gaskell
John A.Gerrard
William Roy Gibbins
Betty Green
Mary Griffin (nee Jones)
Chris Hallinan (Hon.Treasurer E.L.C.C.A.)
Eric J.Haslam
Teresa Hayman
Tommy Hayes (Wrestling)
Ron Hill M.B.E. (Triple Olympian)
Don S.Holt
John Hooson
Derek R.Howarth (Leigh Harriers Hon. Treasurer)
John Hutchinson
Alan J.Isherwood
Michael Latham (Leigh Rugby)
Lionel Lea (Wigan Wheelers)
Edna A.Lee (nee Buxton)
Alf Leonard (Cycling)
Michael Madely
Manchester Wheelers c.c.
Sarah & Tim Marsden
Mary Marsh

Bill McEvoy (Liverpool Harriers)
Iris McKiernan (nee Garfin)
Wilf Morgan (Birchfield Harriers & Historian)
Maurice Morrell (1954 A.A.A. Javelin Champ & Historian)
Marjorie Newton (nee Thorpe)
The late, Fred Norris (Double Olympian)
Edmund Norris
Noreen O'Rourke (nee Gregory)
Dorothy Page (nee Whittaker)
Alan Pennington
Karl Pennington (Wrestling)
Norman C.Pennington (Wrestling)
Bob Philips (Sports Writer)
Jim Prescott
T.C.Ramsdale
Ireen Rankin (nee Rowland)
Eric Ranicar
Eddie J.Rawlinson
Alfred Reid (Cycling)
The late, Marcus Reid (Wrestling)
Peter R.Reid (Wrestling)
Lesley Richards (nee Evans)
John Rigby (Wrestling)
Mary Robinson (nee Hodgson)
The late. Tommy Rothwell (Leigh Rugby)
Jack Sankey (Race Walking)
Bob Shuttleworth (Leigh Rugby)
Neil Shuttleworth (Athletic Historian and
Co-author of Manchester Marathons 1908-2002)
Arnold Simms
Alex Simpson
The late, William G.Simpson
Jack Sixsmith (Cycling)
Norman J.Starkie
Joan Szymanowski (Local Historian)
Philip & Susan Taylor (Authors of J.Dewhurst)
Tony Taylor (Race Walking)
Dennis Thorpe
Dr. Phil Thomas (Sports Writer & Historian)
Hamish M.Thomson (Stockport Harriers & Historian)
Patricia Walmsley (nee Mooney)
British Olympic Association, Wandsworth
Lancashire Public Record Office, Preston
The National Archives, Kew, Richmond, Surrey
Bolton Central Library
Blackpool Central Library
Bury Central Library
Earlestown Newton Library
Leigh Public Library
Liverpool Central Library
Manchester Central Library
St Helens Central Library
Westhoughton Public Library
Wigan Public Library

Should readers notice any errors the publishers will be glad to hear of them, also from anyone who has unpublished photographs of the Leigh Harriers & Athletic Club and its members.

Index

Index

Index

Index

Index

Index

Index

Index

Index

Index

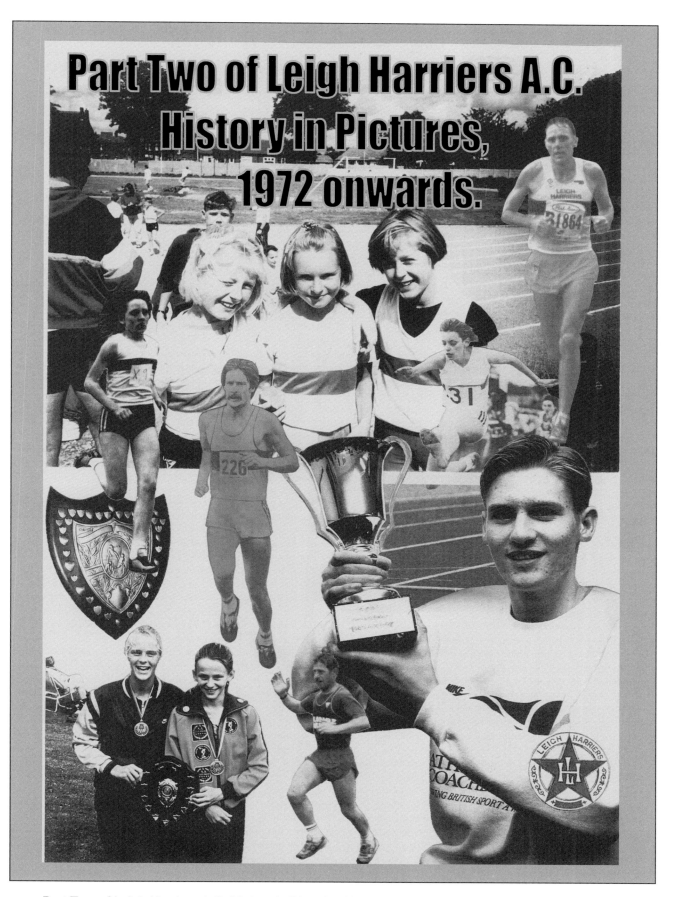

Part Two of Leigh Harriers A.C. History in Pictures 1972 onwards, is currently being compiled and will be available in the near future.